A

life's

journey

FROM

BROOKLYN

TO

NIGERIA

It is required of a man that
he should share the passion
and action of his time at peril
of being judged not to have lived.

Justice Oliver Wendell Holmes, Jr.

A life's journey
FROM BROOKLYN
TO NIGERIA

Alan Feinstein

TRIATLANTIC BOOKS

New York

FOREWORD

My family and I have known of, and later interacted at closed personal level, with Alan and Mary Feinstein for a total of two decades. Initially, I was curious about this Brooklyn-born dentist engaged in the research and later, publication of a two-volume biography of a distinguished Nigerian, Mallam Aminu Kano. The late Aminu Kano has been referred to as the Gandhi of Nigeria - a selfless revolutionary totally dedicated to the upliftment of the masses. The autobiography, *A Life's Journey: From Brooklyn To Nigeria*, provides full insights into the personal odyssey of Alan Feinstein.

The author's background and professional career and even the stint as an officer in World War II, point towards success in later life. And by his own admission, Alan had a good life and a personal good fortune as a result of having Mary for a wife for over 50 years, a fine family, successful children and a decent livelihood from his dental practice. However, for Alan, this was never an end by itself. His life was devoted to a continuous struggle for justice and equity in this turbulent world.

In this regard, it is interesting to note the pointed question which Fred, in his youth, asked his father, "how come you always back the losers?" The fact is that Alan's natural inclination was to be on the side of the underdog and those fighting for political freedom and freedom from want. The prospect of total victory in the immediate or distant future, mattered less to him than the process of struggle itself. In essence, la luta would continua indefinitely, as far as Alan was concerned.

His meeting and subsequent association with Aminu Kano of Nigeria were the defining moments of Alan's political consciousness. This was moreso after Alan's personal disillusionment with the appeal of communism as a central ideology following Khruschev's famous denunciation of Stalin in 1953. His intellectual affinity with and personal devotion to Aminu Kano opened up a whole new vista for Alan. Along with Mary, his indefatigable wife, Alan began their several personal visits to Nigeria to do research, observe events, interview scores of people and generally expanding their circle of friends and contacts in the country. And their residence in New York became the hub of the dinners, contacts and linkages which he organized between African Americans and other Americans on the one hand, and Nigerians temporarily resident in or visiting the United States, on the other.

However, there were small and big disappointments in the relationship between Alan and his adopted country, Nigeria. The Nigerian-American Friendship Society of which he was the founding President, collapsed soon after the holding of a successful international conference. More seriously, Alan felt, until his death, that Nigeria neither lived up to its potentialities nor the vision of his dear friend, Aminu Kano. On the contrary, Nigeria seems to him to be a chaotic country lacking in political direction and remaining in "perpetual transition from military to civilian rule, without even coming close to the path towards democracy which Aminu Kano... has so clearly outlined for his nation". This may be a valid criticism but not even this apparent condition of the Nigerian nation is permanent. Nigeria would fulfil her destiny; what is urgently needed are more committed leaders, political activists and true patriots like Aminu Kano.

Aminu Kano's death devastated Alan who had great difficulties conceiving of a world without his friend. After all, here was a man who, among other things, embodied the national conscience of Nigeria for many years. Alan's consolation was the hope that "the essence of Aminu's life will live on."

Alan Feinstein was an Africanist, a true humanist and his life, ably chronicled in this fine autobiography, would remain an inspiration for all those struggling against socio-economic and political subjugation everywhere. Alan was a good man, a loving family person, a reliable professional and political colleague. He believed that in order to have an exciting and successful life, one needs to be "moral, decent and concerned about others." This troubled world of ours needs the likes of Aminu Kano and Alan Feinstein. It was an appropriate tribute to this multi-dimensional man that the reception for the memorial service in his honor was under the auspices of the Permanent Mission of Nigeria to the United Nations. May his kind and decent soul rest in perfect peace.

Prof. Ibrahim A. Gambari
Ambassador & Permanent Representative of Nigeria
to the United Nations, November 11, 1996.

CONTENTS

PREFACE

It was our first visit to Nigeria, and we had stopped to visit an old friend – a politician named Aminu Kano whom we had met at a party in New York. He was on his way to a political rally, and invited us to tag along.

As we approached the site, our car was engulfed by a surge of his party followers, with clenched fists, and accompanied by shouts of "Am–eee–een! Am–eee–een!" in adoration.

He spoke to the assemblage in his native Hausa, waved a closed umbrella around as though it was a pointing finger, laughed and shouted and we felt as though we understood every word. He spoke in the language of the people, and they understood. He was of them. Cries of "Sawaba!" (freedom) were heard as our car slowly drove off.

Aminu's political party was not the dominant one in his country, but the party he led was in alliance with the ruling party and as such, he had derivative status. However, as we subsequently learned, Aminu's reputation and the respect accorded him extended well beyond his own party and its alliances.

Over the years, we came to understand why Mallam Aminu was widely thought of as the Gandhi of Nigeria. He was a man who tried to change the course of his country; wanted to change people's lives for the better. He definitely changed mine.

This may seem an unlikely statement for a Jewish dentist who grew up in Brooklyn to make. My path has been a winding one, mostly down roads not taken, but they have taken me to people and places I could never have dreamed of in my most creative moments. One such person was Aminu Kano, and one such place was Nigeria.

And therein lies a tale.

— *Alan Feinstein*, New York City, 1995

CHAPTER ONE

THE SHIP'S FOUNDATION

"Choosing to lead the life of a non-conformist radical would present me with a dilemma time and again... I must have been the most conservative radical around, by my own standard as well as that of those around me."

I grew up in Brooklyn, the youngest of the three children of Russian immigrant parents. Until my college years, my whole world had been Jewish. Not in a religious sense, but in the sense that I was always aware of my origins without ever consciously analyzing what being Jewish meant.

We were Jewish, yes, but the question of where I belonged or how I might be different from our Catholic or Protestant neighbors didn't trouble me, until much later. It was the radicalism that emerged in my early years and that came to shape much of my life that became the identity that set me apart.

My association with the sounds and smells and foods of my childhood continues to remain strong, but there was no inner conflict. My choice, at age thirteen, to skip the option offered me to have a bar mitzvah was not an act of separation. It was merely a sign of early teenage rebellion, or perhaps the first indication of my radical rejection of the status quo.

Home to me was a comfortable retreat, but at the same time it was mostly a place to get out of and come back to. It was where we fulfilled responsibility and refueled – dressed, slept and did what we were supposed to do.

My day-to-day contact with my father was slight, but the essence of Pop's basic morality stuck to me: *"Don't do anything to hurt others if you can avoid it; know yourself and don't let vanity misrepresent you to yourself or anyone else; don't do anything of which you'd be ashamed."*

During the years immediately following World War I, my father had developed a profitable import business, dealing with, among other things, the mechanical device that produced Mamma Doll voices. In the late 1920s, tired of fighting off patent infringements by the giants in toy manufacturing, Pop sold his share of the business to a partner – who then held out for patent protection, won the case and later became a multi-millionaire.

Pop reinvested the capital he took out of the company in a real estate deal. Unfortunately, this occurred shortly before the Great Depression descended upon the country. The Crash of 1929 hit our household like a wrecking ball. Pop lost the bulk of his investment.

Memories of the Depression years, which began as I entered my teens, are framed by a stark image of a despondent Pop sitting in the dimly lit living room, playing solitaire day after day, smoking one malodorous cigar after another. Occasionally he would venture out to look at one business opportunity or another, but nothing worked for him in those days.

In 1934 he invested the last of his remaining savings in a retail stationery store. This represented the bottom rung of the entrepreneurial ladder for him. But it was also a business with which he had become familiar as a young Russian emigre. He was deeply American in his own way, a profound believer in the free enterprise system.

Tied to his dream of a comfortable middle-class standard of life was the driving need to provide an education for his children, incorporating perhaps the classic Eastern European Jewish goal of making medical doctors of his sons and marrying his daughter to a professional. (Ultimately, he settled fairly readily for dental school for my brother Leon and myself and accepted, not quite so readily, an insurance man as a spouse for my sister Bea.)

Mom was another breed entirely. She, like Pop, had come to America in her teens from Minsk Gebernya, a province of Czarist Russia. And she, too, valued learning and good breeding, but with a greater emphasis on the latter. Her reverence for education was at once both profound and superficial. She prided herself on her mastery of the English language: Assimilation and social status mattered.

❧

We spent summers at the Mohegan Colony, just north of New York City, where my family had a bungalow. It was there that the first real inner rumblings of pubescence and social conscience became manifest to me. There were many youngsters in the Colony, with a good distribution of ages. We had what were then known as gab fests, often held around campfires that helped us reach out tentatively to our female counterparts. Those sessions included the usual ghost stories and teasing, but it was here that I began to test the political and philosophical waters.

Mohegan was a kind of free wheeling, free-thinking community where families never quite followed the established rules. Through their children, the radical backgrounds of some of the parents began to show. The kids scoffed at religion and taunted me with questions: *"How do you know there's a God? Can you see Him?"* They raised doubts that made me question all my childhood postulates, so when I heard the term agnostic, I embraced it with great relief.

A portent of things to come, in opting for agnosticism I sought what seemed to be the safest middle ground between the faithful and the atheists. "When and if I go," I reasoned, "I won't have to cut all ties." Later, I could never decide what college course to take on registration or what to choose from a menu.

⚜

In high school I began to reach toward that great equalizer, the realm of ideas. Being younger than my classmates, I wasn't as tall or physically developed as they, nor was I as socially adept. But I could still think as well as any of them,and I soon discovered that my age and stage of development was no impediment to expressing myself forcefully. I debated issues with my teachers in social science and history during classroom hours and questioned the validity of our society after hours.

An economics teacher encouraged my tendencies in this direction. His teaching method required at least one active opponent at the student level off whom he could bounce the known economic theories, and I was a willing foil. In his role as master of ceremonies, he could reinforce my ideas or devastate them at his pleasure; but he was good-natured as he opened up my naive, radical ideas for class perusal. I took the bait and enjoyed the combat.

My end term grade was high. Although the instructor's intent in engaging me in debate was to stimulate active discussion in the classroom, the principal effect on me was to infuse me with an inflated opinion of my incompletely formulated concepts. Argument tended to reinforce rather than undermine my ripening radical ideas.

The path from grade school to high school to college and post-graduate levels was assumed and uninterrupted. A choice other than the orderly pursuit of an education simply was not an option in those days. And if one didn't have to be the best, one surely had to be among the best. How else did one make one's mark, fulfill one's raison d'etre?

My protective shell was the ever-expanding frontier of intellectual pursuit. Each new discovery in the realm of ideas was both an immediate thrill – a font of excitement and fulfillment – and a building block for the next and higher formulation. Passionate, irrational love had not yet intruded to confuse my order of things.

By the time I reached my college years, I had come to believe that I could sidestep personal trauma and stress by submerging the events of my life in a higher purpose. I did not expect that my own role in the grand scheme of things would be earth-shaking, but I was confident that strict adherence to an ethical code of conduct and respect for others would, in time, yield the answers.

My entry into Brooklyn College represented a continuation of my adolescent environment, but there my inclination toward radical politics began to take on a somewhat more coherent shape. I found camaraderie in activities organized to raise funds for progressive causes; I joined the local residents in Hungarian and Ukrainian folk dancing at "The Hall"; my friends and I did engage in some struggle concerning the Spanish Civil War, sending one of our number to Spain as an ambulance driver for the Loyalists; and we won a minor skirmish by exposing an anti-Semitic incident in the Village government.

It was at this time, however, that I came to terms with the fact that my devotion to a cause could push me only so far. I could have given up the good life and volunteered my services to the Spanish Loyalist Army, a cause I strongly believed in. Or I could continue to fight for the cause as best I could from a relatively safe perch – as I did. Choosing to lead the life of a non-conformist radical would present me with this dilemma time and again. It seems that from my college years on, I knew where I would go – or rather, where I would not go. Pushed for commitment, I would compromise.

This lack of decisiveness became a pattern for future fateful decisions. I was consistently a man of the middle. The motivation might have been self-preservation or fear – or a stable, placid personality – or perhaps elements of both of the above.

By my senior year I had moved on campus, and with work at the family stationery store reduced to weekends, I had more time to devote to my political pursuits. Brooklyn College by that time had become a fertile field for my radical politics. It was home to the largest chapter of the American Student Union, the national anti-war student organization that was then sprouting up at colleges all over the country.

Living on campus enabled me to merge my social, political and intellectual lives into one. The student union office was home to many a lonely soul who was looking for a similar combination of interests. I found myself proselytizing relentlessly for my radical ideas among the anti-war students. Demonstrations, social, lectures and an endless round of meetings drew willing ears to my arguments.

With my undergraduate years coming to a close, career choices had to be made, and that weighed heavily upon me. The depressing period of my father's unemployment years was still with me, and the need for personal security hovered over my choices. The relative safety of a government job had its allure, but since I was restricted by my economic and cultural background to making a choice among the professions, teaching got top billing.

By this time my brother was in his third year of New York University Dental School, with the tough basic sciences behind him and mostly clinical work ahead, enabling him to continue to help in Pop's store. He loved dental school and urged me to try it. When I was accepted at NYU and faced with the need to make a decision, I came down on the DDS side.

Dentistry, I reasoned, would leave me in some aspect of science, the general field I had always wanted; I could more than likely make a living at it; and I would be left with considerably more leeway for my personal and political life than I might have in medicine, not an inconsequential consideration. And, I would not have a government bureaucracy breathing down my neck.

While characteristically I would ponder long over a dilemma such as deciding which movie to see, this far more momentous decision – a choice of a life work – seemed to come easily. It pleased everyone around me and permitted me to continue in my own pattern, in a familiar environment, with familiar people. Because I consistently feared differentness, avoided extremes and remained a creature of the middle, this career decision fit the pattern.

Although I fancied myself a bold innovator in those days, the brave new paths I followed led me away from introversion but never veered too far from the center. Over the years, I must have been the most conservative radical around, by my own standard as well as that of those around me.

From the beginning, I found it relatively easy to find kindred souls among my fellow dental students to help carry the political torch. We worked through clubs, publications and any other extra-curricular activities appropriate to our goal of improving the lot of humanity and, through this improvement, ultimate liberation through socialism.

In our freshman class of about 125 students, three of us were convinced radicals when we arrived. By the time we graduated four years later, we had twenty to twenty-five colleagues in full agreement with us and a much larger number – close to one half of the class – who were strongly committed progressives.

The core of my own circumscribed world was a triumvirate of friends, a threesome that shared and did most everything together. From this triad we expanded easily on concentric circles, each larger than the last: the radical inner circle, the sympathizers, those beyond that category but still reachable, and then the entire class.

Beyond that were friends of classmates, and finally, the rest of the city and the world. Each circle had a place in our hearts and minds, but as the fields grew wider, they became less personalized, though not necessarily less important to our politically oriented confrere.

In retrospect, the intensity of my ideological involvement through my college and post-graduate years seems to have served for me as a bridge across the adolescent chasm and on into adulthood. Politics gave meaning and purpose to my activities. Moreover, I knew that if all my high-flung ideals were to endure hard testing, the socially useful nature of my chosen profession would still remain.

CHAPTER TWO

LOVE AND WAR

"A war was going on overseas–it hadn't been put on hold for me to straighten out my love life and prepare for my post-war plans."

On December 7, 1941, Pearl Harbor exploded – an event that was followed immediately by the United States' declaration of war against Germany, Japan and the Axis. I was then in the middle of my senior year in dental school. Although my antipathy toward war was almost reflexive by that time, Hitler and his Nazi armies managed to break that down, proving in a way to be a unifying force for us Americans. All of my senior classmates – radical, conservative or in between – lined up in support of this war.

During the initial phase of the war, when neither the Soviet Union nor the U.S.A. was actively engaged, the Communists and their sympathizers categorized the war as phony. Although I, too, accepted this approach at the time, as an anti-fascist and a Jew my latent sympathies were with the Allies.

Dating back to the Spanish Civil War, and before, I had recognized fascists as the devil incarnate, and the complicity of the West in building up and tolerating such a monster had greatly troubled me. It was capitalism's ugliest face. Now, for one of the rare times in my political life, I luxuriated in finding myself on the side of the overwhelming majority. I threw myself into the struggle without reservation.

Along with most of my dental-college classmates, I was excited about entering any branch of the service that would have me. My application for a commission in the all-volunteer navy was turned down when it was discovered that while in an upright position, standing at attention, the distance between my knees measured more than four inches. I was accepted by the U.S. Army, however.

⚜

Shortly after our June 1942 graduation, I found myself at Camp Picket, hop-skip-and-jumping through the eight-week basic training course for all medical officer recruits. From there I was assigned to the 94th Infantry Division, then in the process of formation, first at Fort Custer in Kalamazoo, Michigan, and shortly thereafter at Camp Phillips in Salina, Kansas.

During a three-day weekend in New York City, I arranged to meet up with my two good friends from dental school, one of whom would be arriving directly from a political meeting. He had a very attractive young lady – another participant in the meeting – in tow. As it turned out, Miss Mary Kotick lived near the restaurant where we met, and he and I later walked her home.

Chatting with my friend on the way to my train station, I commented, *"Frustrating, isn't it? Here I meet a lovely gal like that and tomorrow I'm on my way back to Kansas."* He responded off-handedly, *"Why don't you send her a postcard anyway? You've got nothing to lose. Maybe you'll have a date the next time you're home on leave."*

That's exactly what I did, and it yielded that and much more–a luscious, life-long fruit. Our next meeting did not wait for my next home leave. An active and fervent correspondence ensued, culminating in a visit from Mary way out in Salina. She had a month's vacation coming up, and wrote, "Can't make up my mind whether to go to California or Cuba. Of course, if I head west I might be able to stop off in Kansas for a day or two en route. How would that strike you?"

My response: *"Don't suggest something like that unless you mean it. My heart can't take it! Hurry on out."* She stayed the entire month. Thirty days of bliss, at the end of which we were talking marriage. There she was, the apparition of my fantasies materialized in the flesh. I was in seventh heaven and spent every spare minute with her and some that weren't so spare.

Still, I seemed paralyzed by my own indecisive nature. As the months following Mary's first long visit went by, I found myself unmercifully torn between ardor and a wrenching, life-long inability to come down completely and unequivocally on one side of a fence. Finally, in February, nine months after our first meeting, I took control over my wavering convictions and phoned Mary from the officers' club at my new post in Mississippi. I asked her to marry me. She said she would think about it and let me know. She was toying with me, and I deserved it.

We were married in New York on February 13, 1944. Facing the unexpectedly trying behavior of her future in-laws without the on-the-spot fiance to serve as a protective shield,

Mary, almost single-handed, was able to put together a memorable affair on very short notice, to everyone's complete satisfaction. And has been functioning in like fashion for our subsequent five decades together.

⚜

Meanwhile, back at the army post, an infantry division was in training, from scratch, for a war going on overseas. It hadn't been put on hold for me to straighten out my love life and prepare for my post-war plans. I was assigned to the division artillery responsible for the dental health of four artillery battalions and a headquarters company.

This army experience was my first intimate contact with the America that wasn't influenced directly by New York and New Yorkers. I moved cautiously in those early army years, not knowing how to approach these creatures from outer space, the other U.S.A., about which I knew so little. I felt instinctively that the approach to my new associates had to be more restrained than that followed in my closer-to-home undergraduate and dental college years, but what was the correct course if I wanted to maximize my influence on events and opinions and at the same time continue to have warm relations with those about me?

It was my perception that a retreat on the question of racial equality would have been a blow to our collective war effort, as well as to my overall humanist goals. Instead, I believed, an aggressive and open struggle for human rights was called for. The pitfall to avoid was embarrassment to the forces in the government that were honestly attempting to wage the war efficiently toward a successful conclusion.

But as my notes of May 24, 1943, stated:

This army business is quite a bit more complex than it would seem on the surface. Why not just agitate at every opportunity for a quick victory and unity on national, international and racial bases? Sounds simple enough, but it is in the application of this formula that complexities arise. Should I raise such issues as pro-trade unionism at all times to all people? Racial equality? I would like to, but would that be correct? ...

To cut off a discussion in order to avoid confrontation would interrupt the continuity of one's argument. To go too fast would be isolating. ... In a factory or on the campus, a homogenous well-knit group united against an obvious and common foe would tend to stimulate open, uninhibited discussion and organization around action for mutual benefit. In an army camp we similarly can reason, but more often than not, we have to busy ourselves in explaining why there isn't action.

I presume that the situation will change when in active combat. Would there be any difficulty engaging a soldier who has seen action in conversation about the purposes of the war? When black and white fall alongside of one another, won't that alter a racist's attitudes? ... Caution must be exerted by the progressive soldier trying to retain the respect of the G.I. and proselytize at the same time. It is clear that patience is essential, for progress here is necessarily slow.

⁂

Shortly after D-Day, our division had just about completed its training and had been put on alert for overseas action. I was called to headquarters to be handed orders transferring me to a combat engineer group. I was furious. I was sure that I was being transferred out to avoid my serving in active combat overseas.

I knew that despite glowing reports from the division artillery surgeon, from the division dental surgeon, and from headquarters staff, recommendations for my promotion were turned down regularly. (It wasn't until I was transferred out of the division that my promotion went through without a hitch.)

I was also aware that a thorough background check of my political past had yielded an army intelligence assessment that I was "probably a Communist sympathizer." My father had been told by friends and neighbors that I must be in line for a promotion, because the army had been around asking questions about me.

At the same time, several of my fellow officers in the division, each in turn, had pulled me aside furtively to tell me that G-2 had been around asking questions, but that each of the officers so questioned had reassured them that I was "normal" and a patriotic American.

Moreover, I had traveled from my unit, stationed in Mississippi at the time to Atlanta, Georgia, for three days of interrogation by the investigative division, but nothing conclusive came out of that incident either. It was during this time of intensive undercover examination of my political views that the following melodramatic notations were made in my occasional notebook:

April 1, 1944

The more I examine my personal beliefs and their relationship to the war effort, the more incongruous that relationship seems. Here I am, embroiled in a conflict of life and death, consciously contributing my best to that effort, consistently asking for overseas duty, and attempting to maintain a high fighting spirit and morale, and instill it in all my immediate associates.

In the face of this, perhaps even because of it, I am considered dangerous. As a reward for such effort, I am being investigated by army intelligence. An unswerving fighter against fascism, I will probably be placed in a position where I can do the least good for the war effort ...

Last week I attended a lecture espousing the cause of national and international unity, roundly condemning loose lips, rumors and anti-racial feelings as divisive and unpatriotic. Then I went to the post movie house to see "Moscow Strikes Back," showing the most significant contribution of the U.S.S.R. to the war effort. This week I receive a questionnaire from G-2 division asking me if I "ever worked for a foreign government.". . .

It might be worth noting here that the sometime diary of my war years has a number of sentences blocked or torn out, testifying to the contradictory and confused attitude our government and army had toward its radical allies of the moment and our fears as a result.

When I received my transfer orders, I rushed to take my bitter complaints to my artillery headquarters superiors, eliciting their deep sympathy but little else. A recounting of the process whereby my transfer took place revealed that my new outfit, a combat engineer group, was not only alerted for overseas action but was actually leaving for the Port of Embarkation the day after I was scheduled to join it.

When they lost a dental officer to illness at the last moment, the army turned to our division for a replacement. So I was it. I was much relieved after that explanation, for I realized that in this case, preventing me from seeing active combat was not the motivation behind my transfer.

My personal involvement with the investigative branch of the army had embittered me, but didn't particularly slow up my career thereafter. The officers of the engineer group welcomed me with open arms and laughed sympathetically when my record eventually caught up with me.

CHAPTER THREE

ARMY DENTIST

*"I became aware that the engineer combat battalions assigned to
our group were manned principally by segregated
African-American troops and their white American officers..."*

One day after I joined the combat engineers, we were off to
Rhode Island and our port of embarkation. The first weekend
there I was permitted out of the restricted zone and down to
New York City and my wife. The second weekend Mary
arranged to come to Providence, but by the time she arrived I
was on the high seas. It was fourteen months before we saw
one other again. Leaving my bride of four months had me rue-
ful, but I was elated and high as a kite on another level,
scared of what was ahead of me.

We landed on the Normandy shore three weeks after D-
Day and raced across France, reaching the city of Nancy in

Alsace-Lorraine one day after our forces recaptured it from the Germans. Coming in from a succession of field bivouacs, we welcomed our new quarters in a high-rise apartment house that had been used by the Germans as a headquarters.

In my role as a member of the medical detachment, I moved about more or less independently, carrying the foot-powered drill and other equipment that a dentist needed to function in an open field. Accompanied by a technician, I travel to a field or clearing in the woods near the headquarters of one or another of our attached battalions. We would remain a few days, take care of any emergencies, and move on to the next area. On several occasions when our headquarters billets were in or attached to a village that was populous enough to have had a dentist, I would temporarily appropriate his office and work out of it until our next forward move.

I had found just such an office, with two treatment rooms, while in Bavaria. There the German dentist (who had not fled as we advanced), using the pretext of helping me find the appropriate equipment and materials, was able to hover over me and keep an eye on his property. At one point, with a slightly embarrassed but worried smile on his face, he wondered if my dental assistant's black skin color would rub off on his precious instruments! It was astonishing to me that a man with his education (and in an applied science at that) could have been so taken in by the Nazi racist propaganda.

The worst casualty our medical detachment suffered was an ambulance pock marked with bullet holes when it ventured up to and beyond the front line to contact one or several of our attached engineer battalions. However, the small headquarters company to which we were attached, consisting of sixty or so soldiers, did suffer the loss of four men and a jeep when they went forward to find our next billet and found themselves ambushed by Germans instead. After VE Day we learned that two of them had been killed and the other two taken prisoner.

The omnipresent confrontation with death was given a ghoulish twist one day when I sighted a truck loaded with corpses heading back from the front. Distressing enough unto itself, it became so much more so when I noticed its bumper insignia: 94th Division. How many of my buddies from the 94th were in that truck? I shuddered, and later learned that the division's first active combat encounter had wreaked severe havoc, with many, many casualties.

❧

The confidence that the officers in the engineer combat group had placed in me was demonstrated when, in addition to my usual dental responsibilities, I was charged with the duties both of postal officer, censoring mail, and information and education officer, supervising the imparting of morale-building and political information to the troops.

As information and education officer for the engineer group, I really felt I could shine. Political education and morale building: just up my alley. I prepared lectures meticulously and tried to stimulate audience participation. I used the printed material sent directly from Washington sources, of which there was an ample supply.

The information and education assignment assumed greater significance for me when I became aware that the engineer combat battalions assigned to our group were manned principally by segregated African-American troops and their white American officers, with a generous sprinkling of southern crackers (whose tradition in the army could be placed back for several generations).

I had to face the ire of several of those officers on more than one occasion for arranging lectures on democracy and

racism. It didn't matter to them that I used only official literature sent from Washington for that very purpose. These old-
line officers were sure that my discussion of these matters
would adversely affect the discipline of their troops.

On more than one occasion our differences blew up into
real controversy. Every time I was accused of heresy or Red
propaganda, I could whip out one government pamphlet or
another to prove I was on the side of the angels, and they
could only sputter. A couple of them even begrudgingly
modified their positions along the way. Most did not.

National policy at that point in history was somewhat
ambivalent. Washington didn't know how to handle our
alliance with the Soviet Union, or our heavy reliance on
African-Americans as combat engineers and transportation
troops. The conflict in which I was personally involved,
seemed however, to have arisen less from the Washington
directives and more from the subversion of those directives as
they passed on down through the chain of command.

ᘒᕲᕲᕲᕲ

Contact with this engineer combat group, as well as with
the other two outfits with which I served, was, however, a
real eye-opener for me. I realized how much I could learn
from the southerners and midwesterners, those with rural
as well as urban backgrounds. My single-minded devotion
to my ideals had me hewing pretty close to the path I was
following when I entered the army. Since I was so sure of
the superiority of my views, I thought of myself as more of
a teacher than a student.

As postal officer it was my duty to read all outgoing mail
to ensure that no security information leaked out. I came
across very little to censor – an occasional place name or

troop numbers – but I did find the experience a significant learning process.

African-Americans, some with limited education and even less exposure to the outer world, were writing their buddies and loved ones back home, revealing their escapades in contact with white Europeans, and French or German women, in graphic terms. In Germany our official non-fraternization policy held little meaning for these newly exposed.

Titillation, sometimes vengeful and sometimes awestruck, dominated their responses. There were a few who, giving vent to the pent-up anger of generations of mistreatment, personalized each sexual contact as a racial conquest. The usual and not unexpected boasting of the macho G.I. was magnified for them by this distorted lifting of the color barrier.

The expression of these emotions and experiences in colorful so-called black English moved me, as well as confused me. The intimate contact with what I recognized then as a culture totally different from my own made me question how universal were my previous perceptions of an international culture. An awareness of my Euro-centricity was beginning to penetrate.

Some time later, during the immediate postwar years, this exposure to the realities of life outside of my narrow New York urban orbit led me to a distressful confrontation. I had organized and was attending a class on race relations when the teacher arbitrarily dismissed army statistics which revealed a high rate of venereal disease and disciplinary problems among black troops as a racist canard.

She recommended a course of action that would deny and dismiss these figures out of hand. From the floor of the classroom, I timidly tried to modify her strong but unsubstantiated views. I pointed out that there were am-

Dental School, 1942

In the army, 1943

ple sociological explanations for this behavior and suggested that a more effective approach would be to work toward raising the educational and economic levels of the troops. Given a greater stake in the society, personally ruinous or generally anti-social behavior, where it did exist, might be modified.

The sky fell on my head. I was a bourgeois apologist for all that was evil in our society. The instructor was particularly incensed when no one in the class rose to defend her position, and several other veterans present, including one African-American, rose to defend mine. The controversy raged on, long after extensive two- and three-person meetings and discussions were held in an effort to persuade one or the other of us to modify our position.

⚜

As the war approached its end, I was transferred to a quartermaster battalion stationed back in Metz. Here too, the adjustment to my new outfit was relatively quick and easy. My paranoia about my political background was alleviated somewhat by the attitude that prevailed in our now primarily civilian army. The 273rd Quartermaster Battalion had not had a dentist assigned to it for some time, so my acceptance on that level was quick and spontaneous.

Then too, somehow an army dentist had a specially favored position. At the lower echelons, if a soldier did his assigned job well his past was ignored. Idiosyncratic behavior in a dentist could be readily excused, with the standards of soldiering applied to others somehow lowered for us. This made life a lot easier for me.

At the time, Metz was much further away from the front lines and, as a consequence, more relaxing. I could wander about the city when not at work, which I did. While exploring the city's nooks and crannies off the beaten track, I came across a storefront headquarters for the Communist Party of the Metz Region. An irresistible urge to speak with anyone I could find inside pushed me to open the door and introduce myself to the several Frenchmen seated there. A roundtable discussion in my schoolroom French ensued, bantering in tone but earthy enough for me to be moved by their details of their underground activity as guerrilla fighters during the occupation.

A few weeks later I was sent back to Paris to participate in a week-long course for information and education officers. I was pleased to hear that Edouard, the education director and number two man for the Communist Party of the Metz Region, was to be in Paris at the same time for a course of his own.

I was proud of my progress in French by this time, and displayed it uninhibitedly while strolling all over town with Edouard, who knew not a word of English. There was much to talk about, for Jacques Duclos, the head of the French Communists, had openly attacked the American Party under Earl Browder for what he called "right wing deviation." He was referring to the attempt of the American party to establish an independent line, based more closely on American history, while projecting the possibility of a period of class peace and a peaceful postwar co-existence for socialist and capitalist nations, based on the Teheran Agreements.

We walked up and down *les rues de Paris*, sat and sipped the strong French coffee and argued, each defending his own country's position. At the end of the day, we bade each other *adieu*, readily agreeing that it was the inadequacy of my French applied to these deeper abstract and philosophical concepts that made the gap between us seem wider than it really was. Little did we dream that the gap was a rift that would widen to earthquake proportions in the postwar decades.

❦

The sudden death of President Franklin Delano Roosevelt on the eve of his greatest triumph shook me and the world to our roots. We had had thirteen years of depression, recovery, war and approaching peace with him, and hardly knew the U.S.A. with any other chief. I feared for the nation, but knew that those of us who survived would have a relatively complete victory and would be able to move on.

At the time of FDR's death, our outfit had reached the environs of Nuremburg, deep in Bavaria, with events pointing clearly to the imminent total destruction of the Nazi armies. There was still concern about the possibility of trans-shipment to the Pacific Front, but that possibility seemed remote. We began to anticipate a return to the states.

Finally, we were on our way home, thirteen months after my hectic departure for overseas duty. Though the westbound ocean voyage was considerably more direct than the zig-zagging we went through on our eastbound Atlantic crossing, it took about the same twelve days, because the ship's engines were in need of an overhaul and consequently were run at half speed. I passed the time of day sitting on the deck of the ocean liner, fantasizing about what my life back home would be if and when I ever got out of the service.

We did not know what awaited us after we docked. Trans-shipment to the Pacific was still a possibility, especially for medical officers who were excluded from the point system that would earn state-side service or honorable discharges for others. Imagine our elation when August 14th, the day we landed on the Brooklyn docks, turned out to be VJ Day.

We were immediately dispatched to a camp in nearby New Jersey, where I rushed to a telephone at the first opportunity. While awaiting my turn, I relished the surprise and excitement I would arouse when Mary heard me say, "Hi, Hon', I'm home." Instead, I was rocked back on my heels when, before I could open my mouth I was greeted with, "Darling, where were you? I've been waiting all day for your call."

The top-secret travel orders I had been censoring out of all mail communications for a year had been easily cracked by my wife's initiative and persistent doggedness! She had known the exact date and time of my arrival, but discreetly had avoided greeting me at the dock out of concern that I might object to her being the only greeter, thus exposing me to suspicion. A neat foretaste of her prowess at getting things done with dispatch when she deemed it necessary or desirable – which was most of the time.

The conclusion of the war in the Pacific had changed the entire picture. Not knowing how to handle us, the bureaucracy gave us all the thirty-day furloughs that were due us, and said that we would be notified of further orders upon our return to the post. I hurriedly hopped a train bound for Mary's tiny apartment in midtown Manhattan, my home-to-be when the army decided they had had enough of me.

I think of that moment when I met Mary in the downstairs hall, as she was returning from a brief food shopping tour, as one of the most exciting of my life up to that point and since. My whole life flashed through my mind. Flashbacks, not only of the year just passed, but of the long-ago days as well, were mingled with my fantasies and dreams of what was ahead. Everything new: wife, life, profession, location, family-to-be, all to be integrated into our struggle for a better world.

⁜

Before I realized it, my month was up and I was back in the dental clinic in Camp Lee, Virginia, awaiting new orders. Impatient with the inevitable delays involved in the demobi-

Combat engineers, 1945, in France

Reading *War and Peace*, 1943

lization period, I extended a weekend leave in order to visit the Surgeon General's office in Washington. My plan was to request assignment to a six-month dental internship being offered at Walter Reed Hospital near Washington, D.C. Much to my surprise, I was asked, "Do you want that assignment or would you rather get out of the army as surplus?" I quickly answered, "If I have that choice, I'll take a discharge." I was told that my discharge orders would be processed within the next few days.

Incredulous, I returned and timidly recounted my experience to the other dentists hanging around the clinic. But in a day or two when my name appeared on the discharge list, effective immediately, with a two-month terminal leave, they were all convinced I had considerably more influence in Washington than I had let on.

The few weeks head start I had on the others as a result of my initiative turned out to be a real boon, for office space was at a premium in midtown Manhattan where I wanted to practice. An ad in the New York Times offered a practice for sale on Madison Avenue, in the Grand Central area, for a paltry two or three thousand dollars – little enough, even considering the decrepit equipment and the absence of a practice with it.

The dental units were quite functional and could easily be replaced as it became necessary and feasible. The rent was controlled by law. I was practicing in short order and eking out a living from the day I started my practice. My classmates and military colleagues in dentistry were delayed for months in getting started, had significantly greater start-up expenses, and in many cases had to compromise on location.

Life for me began anew.

CHAPTER FOUR

A PROGRESSIVE PRACTICE

"The overarching concern of my life was to be socio-political.
All my personal good fortune was to be integrated
as part of the struggle, not an end unto itself."

Up to the day of my discharge from the service, it seemed that I had been merely preparing to live. My early years had been defined by the various schools I attended, from elementary school on through high school, college and dental college – a story not too different from that of others with the same class background. Even the army years – an extraordinary departure – were not so extraordinary when seen as the shared experience of others of my generation.

Now, suddenly, I was about to pass through the gates and savor the real thing. All the prerequisites were present: a wife, a profession and good health-made meaningful by a mantle of social purpose.

The overarching concern of my life was still to be socio-political. All of my personal good fortune was to be integrated as part of the struggle, not an end unto itself. I was set upon following my intense devotion to an ideal color-blind society of equal rights and opportunities for all to its logical conclusion, come what may.

In retrospect, that complete dedication seems to have been more a starry-eyed vision, part of a pattern that had been developing all my life. Wherever the struggle was joined, my ideals remained intact, but somehow I consistently felt more comfortable with a middle and safer path than in the role of the wild-eyed radical I fancied for myself.

Remember that I chose to fight the Spanish Civil War as a loyal auxiliary on the U.S. home front – while faithfully preparing for my personal career – rather than as a battle-front volunteer. During the three and a half years I was in the military, including a year under fire with a sharply focused vision of a detestable fascist enemy ever in front of me, I seemed better able to face danger. I must add, however, that even these circumstances never really called for firm individual initiative on my part.

⁂

In the immediate post-war period, when I returned to civilian life, I remained most comfortable and most effective in the safer organizations with broad memberships, so-called mass organizations.

I wanted to participate in the broad-based veterans groups, to help veterans get what I felt they deserved from our government, and open left-wing political views obviously would have isolated me. I was Jewish and that was isolating enough when I chose to join the local American Legion Post rather than the more left leaning AVC (American Veterans Committee).

Nonetheless, I was able to build a less-than-intimate, but still respectful, relationship with my fellow vets, to the point where I became housing chairman, county delegate, and the like. Despite my apparent success in that milieu, political progress seemed much too slow even for my patient, tolerant mode. To offset this and use up my reservoir of political energy, I assumed an active role in the nitty-gritty politics of the community.

The juxtaposition of my efforts on behalf of veterans' rights in the American Legion and my activities in the neighborhood never seemed a contradiction to me.

When all is said and done, the worthiness of my activities in the broader based organizations was all that remained for me to hold on to when the scale tilted so disastrously later in the mid 1950s.

At the same time, Mary was contributing her impressive organizational talents to building the American Labor Party, an independent, broadly liberal third party with some status in New York City and state. Communist influence within that party was strong, but as that influence became dominant, a segment of the leadership split off to form yet another statewide party, the Liberal Party. Ultimately, it survived and the original ALP did not.

༄

At this point, it would seem in order to ruminate a bit about past and current attitudes toward the Communists – my own attitude, that of my circle of friends and acquaintances and that of the populace in general. (It's probably obvious that when my Brooklyn College professors used to call me "Red," they weren't just talking about the color of my hair.) My complete dissociation from the Communists some time down the line was to be a severely traumatic experience for me, extending over a period of years. But to skirt the details of my connections at that time would be to omit a defining part of my life.

There are those of the next generation who might have difficulty comprehending the emotional upheaval we lived through during those years, when the epithet "Communist" raised a whole complex of responses: denial when one wanted to maintain a relationship on an even keel; disgust at the lack of understanding on the part of the accuser; self-defense when one considered the distortion of the concept over the years; and finally, self-examination to better understand why and how we came to associate with the radical movement and how we have evolved since.

It is said, perhaps frivolously but nonetheless pretty truthfully, that in my generation over half the intellectuals and literati in America passed through the Communist Party, or were among its fellow travelers, at one time or another during their lives. When, during the early 1950s, the gruesome McCarthy inquisition, with its venomous attacks, grew to a frenzied hysteria, fear of being associated with the nation's radical fringe seeped down to a large part of the population, and Communist influence rapidly waned.

Looking for a "Red under the bed" became a preoccupation of so-called patriots, with the rest of the population intimidated into denying jobs or contacts to any left-wing adherents, or even those with merely liberal ideas. Those who agreed, even to the slightest degree, with the egalitarian, humanistic ideals promulgated by the Communists of the day lived in fear of persecution. There was also the concern among the more dedicated that in such an atmosphere, even being identified as so-called fellow travelers would isolate them and limit their effectiveness.

Under these circumstances, there is an understandable dilemma for a left winger wanting to delve into his past. As I struggle to accurately trace the evolution of my thinking, I hesitate to detail it. A strong residue of this McCarthy-type thinking remains to this day, even after the revelations of the Twentieth Congress in the USSR and the eventual collapse of the international Communist world.

Having been a sympathizer still carries a taint. But the context of the times (long before the sudden and unpredicted collapse of Communism through *perestroika* and *glasnost*) was unique. Until the McCarthy inquisition cast a pall over the nation, this form of radicalism was widely considered to be a legitimate ideological alternative, counterpoised to that of conservative free enterprise.

When I, or anyone, speak about past involvement, there are inevitably others implicated who might very well be upset by revelations about their past. In the name of frankness and honesty, does a writer have the duty or right to expose others, without their permission, to the scrutiny of the unwitting or vacuous?

These are very complex matters, and I must ask myself: Is paranoia involved? Are the motivation and humanistic idealism that were then considered to be the underpinnings of the Communist movement comprehensible to an audience decades later? Any reconstruction of this period is emotional at best, imbued with experiences internalized, possible regret at having been taken in by what we chose to read or listen to, and an ongoing desire to continue to make a social contribution during what remains of a lifetime.

⚜

As my fellow dentists and I emerged from the highly structured, completely encompassing military establishment, we had to find our own individual niches in a society at peace. Two or three of us conceived of a plan to bring top-notch but low-cost dentistry to the workers. Our concept was to approach trade-union leaders to encourage them to refer their members to us for treatment. Payment was to be by a fixed annual charge per member, or a low fee for service, or a combination of the two. They were to set up an office or offices at a central location, or, if they preferred, we would use our private offices.

We were well ahead of our time. Third-party payment for dental care was non-existent and was still in its infancy for medical treatment. The insurance professionals we consulted told us that the basic principle of health insurance at acceptable cost was for the well to pay for the ill; the problem with our concept was that the two major dental diseases, caries and periodontal disease, occurred more frequently than any other. Almost everyone is dentally ill. In other words, they said it wouldn't work.

After a short time, the number of dentists in our plan had expanded to eight. The closeness we had developed as fellow activists during four intense years in dental school was to continue into the postwar years or so we thought. The gloomy predictions of our insurance advisors didn't stop us. Quality couldn't be compromised, but we could cut costs by sharing expenses and accepting modest incomes.

However, we hadn't counted on the response of the trade-union leaders. A more short-sighted lot we couldn't find. The quality of the work didn't interest them, only cutting costs. And they didn't mind cutting the dentists' incomes to the bone to get there. Their approach most closely resembled that of the farmer who fed his horse less and less each day to save money. Just as he finally succeeded in cutting out the horse's food altogether, the horse died.

So we dickered with the trade union officials and weeks passed. The first of our eight dentists decided to pull out. He already had an established practice, since he had been rejected by the armed forces for medical reasons. He decided his political work superseded his professional work. He wanted to continue spending half his time on the phone doing political work, and the other half caring for those patients who would put up with this.

The next one to leave had found a practice for sale and just couldn't wait any longer. With no resolution in sight, the project fell apart. Many years later we were approached by some of the same union leaders to set up a clinic such as the one we had proposed, but of course we were all completely committed elsewhere by that time. Our idealism had fallen by the wayside when it met with hard reality.

Over the next ten years four of us continued our joint effort to provide quality low-cost professional care by associating an office with a medical health insurance plan group out of Brooklyn. Each of us worked the equivalent of one day a week in that office, while devoting the remainder of our time to our own private practices.

While this was going on, my Manhattan practice had blossomed. It had come along easier than expected, even though patients didn't drop in to a dental office located on the eighteenth floor of a midtown office building with eighteen dentists plying their profession in my building alone. Growth depended more on referrals and the network for those referrals, for me, was widespread. I spread myself even further by joining a dental panel which supplied low-fee basic dental care for recently arrived refugees. Though the fees paid by the refugee organization didn't even cover costs, the work became a fertile source for further referrals. As a result my practice took off quickly, yielding a comfortable, if not lavish, living almost from the start.

I did enjoy my practice. My location and personal contacts produced a heterogeneous grouping of patients; well-to-do, working class and poor, ecumenical, black and white, young and old and in-between. That was just what this doctor had ordered. I loved the intimate personal one-on-one contact and the respect shown me by the people who came through the office, whether as patient or fellow worker. The office atmosphere was relaxed, and immediate payment for service was never a requirement.

CHAPTER FIVE

HOME AND POLITICS

"As had been the case in the military, ... I knew that if I revealed my leftist background, my effectiveness would be greatly diminished."

Although it was not our intention to make dentistry my primary focus, continuing education had to be part of a self-imposed regimen. To function as a competent practitioner required extensive study time. This study time in the form of lectures, meetings and courses as well as professional reading, when added to my political preoccupation, left little time for Mary and me to build our lives together.

I don't think however, that lack of time was responsible for what marital difficulties we had. Actually I don't even think of them as marital difficulties.

Rather, it was more of a merger of two different and strong personalities living under one roof, each with specific gifts and needs. No matter how much we had in common, this still required some adjustment.

Early in our courtship, while still in an army camp in Salina, Kansas, in the flush of the excitement of an emerging, durable relationship, I inadvertently let slip a comment: "You know, there may be a period of infatuation during a courtship, but I don't think that people really fall in love until after they are married." The comment was inadvertent, not because it lacked validity, but because of its bad timing. We were already so deeply committed, Mary reasoned, how could we not be in love?

As we grew closer over our first few years together, I think she came around to my point of view. It was only after the maturing of our lives together, only after we learned pretty much all there was to learn about one another and still found qualities that were positive enough to warrant the many adjustments we each had to make, that we could say we had found love and happiness together.

I must say that at first I went blithely on my own way without realizing that much of what I was doing – or not doing – was creating stress in my wife. But soon enough I found myself walking on eggs. Why don't you bring flowers home? Why aren't you aware of its effect on others when you do or say something thoughtless? Why do I have to tell you? You should know you're offending without my telling you.

Mary's sensitivities and my insensitivity seemed to be at the core of whatever came between us during those early years. Her strength and unbending will to get things done were, in a way, also a weakness. Although I am more relaxed than she, that too represented both strength and weakness. I was almost always the unwitting offender and Mary the offended.

During those years, proving the other to be at fault assumed disproportionate importance, but it gradually became clear to us that there was no line dividing right from wrong. We were not right or wrong, but just different personalities. Gradually I offended less and she felt less offended. And we lived happily ever after.

Mary's intense involvement in people's lives when the spirit moved her, her fervor, boundless energy and ability to unhesitatingly tackle any and all situations got us where I would not otherwise have dared to go, while my unflappable, quiet personality seemed to provide the stability and security that served us both so well.

Our personalities are as opposite as can be found in any two people, and after fifty years of marriage neither of us changed very much. Mary: bombastic, energetic and never passive; intrusive, interested in what makes those around her tick, but also wanting to help them live up to their potential (as she sees it, of course). Spirited! Alan: groping, consistent and reliable. Mary for the jump start and get up and go, bordering on pushiness; Alan, thorough-going, always a willing participant, rarely the initiator, analytic and looking for resolution, bordering on the prosaic.

❦

After a year of this brand of togetherness, we were ready in 1947 to think about children. As part of Mary's ALP activities she was asked to take on a major responsibility as a sector manager in one of several of Vito Marcontonio's congressional campaigns. We decided to undertake both tasks simultaneously. We were lucky on both scores. Mary got pregnant immediately, and Vito Marcantonio was elected with her help.

The impending arrival of our first offspring brought with it the problem of finding a bigger apartment. Mary's antennae were raised and somewhere along the line she located an elderly woman, living alone in a really broken down but (for

With Fred at three months old,
1947

Nancy and Fred, 1954

Passport photo with Mary, Nancy
and Fred, 1960

her) much too large townhouse in Greenwich Village. After some cajoling and stroking, she hesitatingly accepted Mary's solution to her problem and ours: a swap. Our tiny apartment with minimal rent (thirty-two dollars a month – astounding in retrospect) could serve her needs, and we would take the townhouse off her hands.

Those of our friends and relatives who saw the place before we moved in thought we were mad. My father shook his head and almost refused to lend us the money we needed for the reconstruction. "How can you think of raising kids on the streets of Greenwich Village?" We had to repair holes in the walls and floors, repair broken windows and keep a coal-fired heating unit going all night. Pregnant Mary didn't hesitate a moment. The $5,000 we sank into our living quarters on the two ground floors to make it habitable hardly seemed to make a difference, but when amortized over our three-year-lease period, it came to only $135 per month.

The upper two floors were available for sublet, which we proceed to do, covering all our other costs (rent and mainte-nance), leaving only this amortization as our total cost – an acceptable level. With a lease extension we ended up living there for eight years, thereby reducing our rental costs to one-third of our original estimate. And we had a seven-room apartment in which to raise our two kids.

The year 1947 was a momentous one for us. It was the month of June when it all happened. We completed our move on June 20th. Cars were at a premium in those years, but we managed to get hold of a Buick convertible (second hand) on June 25th. And then the crowning glory! Our son, Fred, arrived on June 27th.

Three years later our second child, Nancy, was conceived in the midst of similar turmoil. Our duplex apartment in Greenwich Village was more than ample in size, but there were some awfully cold winters. I had to get up at 6:00 a.m. to stoke the furnace so that it would be reasonably warm when the household rose. Even so, on more than one occasion we had to crack the ice in the bassinet in order to bathe the children. This, in the heart of downtown Manhattan.

⚜

Within months of our move to Greenwich Village, the Henry Wallace campaign for President went into full swing. With our relocation, my East Midtown American Legion activity had come to a halt. I was quickly immersed in the organization of a Manhattan Vets For Wallace Committee, but we never did get very far. With the disappointing debacle of the 1948 election, I realized that a national third party was not in the offing for some time to come. Instead, I found myself in the local Democratic Party club during the ensuing years. Mary continued with her ALP activities, just moving over to the Village chapter.

Since neither my status as a bona-fide World War II veteran nor my status as a Jew had expired yet, I hooked up with the local Jewish War Veterans. The membership approved of my constant push for active involvement, and it wasn't long before I became commander of the post. In turn, my standing and prestige as commander enabled me to approach the Greenwich Village Association to co-sponsor a community-wide meeting during Brotherhood Week. My suggestion that a First Annual Brotherhood Award be given to a local minister who shared the premises of his church with a rabbi and his synagogue was received well.

During the next few years the brotherhood award and meeting became an accepted and much anticipated event in the Village. Charles Abrams, the housing specialist, Jackie Robinson the you-know-who, and Borough President Stanley

Visiting Czechoslovakian family, 1959,
with Nancy and Fred

In the home of friends in Japan, with Fred and Mary, 1963

Isaacs, a strong fighter for human rights, were among the more noted of the recipients. After a while, under the pretext of restricting the award to local civic leaders, a succession of neighborhood activists were honored, more as an acknowledgment of their involvement in local politics than as active proponents of an open-ended melting pot.

And so, over the years, my interest in both the Brotherhood Committee and the Jewish War Veterans waned. As I saw it, the value of the annual meeting was in influencing the participants to apply the platitudes expressed there to their daily activities. But over time it had become more of a political football to be used by civic-minded but ambitious individuals and special-interest groups. These included the local Tamawa Democratic Club, which was serving as the Greenwich Village base for Carmine DeSapio, the Tammany boss at the time.

Besides, as I tired of my role as a semi-professional veteran and Jew, I felt less and less comfortable in these groups. This was not where I saw my real core identity. I was a conscious political animal, and though I certainly regarded these activities as worthwhile contributions to humanity and the ultimate goal of the Marxist (which is, of course, "To each according to his need, from each according to his ability"), they were still a long way removed from that goal.

I allowed myself to change the focus of my interest to the Reform Democratic Club in the adjacent neighborhood, Chelsea. There I continued to actively volunteer my services, this time ending up as a Democratic County Committeeman and a member of the Tilden Club's Civil Rights Committee. I emerged from the years following my involvement with the Village Brotherhood Committee with a photo taken with Jackie Robinson to show my children and grandchildren, and greatly enhanced recognition as a public-spirited citizen.

My instinct was to find the people-oriented issues in any broad organization within which I worked. Even in the most pragmatic of political organizations, the neighborhood political club – where the opportunistic climbers and sycophants congregated – the ostensible purpose of the organization was to better the lot of humanity. Since I had no personal political ambitions, I would ferret out the activities that helped reach toward this ideal: civil rights and liberal programs.

In a naive, ill-considered way, I believed that if any civil libertarian anxious to achieve these lofty goals took action to achieve them, he or she would progress naturally toward the next logical stage, which in my mind was a socialist orientation. I was actually stunned to discover the level of devotion and sincere commitment to the cause of civil liberties held by fellow committee members who, at the same time, harbored strongly negative opinions toward socialists and Marxists.

As had been the case in the military, without stopping to consider the implications, I knew that if I revealed my leftist background, my effectiveness would be greatly diminished. But the realization that these attitudes toward socialist thought existed in otherwise liberal organizations was a real eye-opener and must have been the imperceptible beginning of the end for me. Although I surely did not see it in those terms at the time.

CHAPTER SIX

THE PEEKSKILL CONCERT

"We were personally face to face with politically violent behavior directed against us in our own country for the first time in our lives."

My eyes were opened in a different way in the summer of 1949 when I was involved in organizing a concert near our summer home in the Mohegan Colony in Westchester. We summered in the little cottage that had belonged to my father, with Mary and me commuting to New York City by train. The change of venue was no occasion for respite from political involvement, and we focused our activities on fundraising and cultural proselytizing through activities like lectures and concerts.

One such event was an annual concert by Paul Robeson, the well-known athlete, singer, actor and radical political activist, for the benefit of the left-wing Civil Rights Congress.

By 1949, the character of Mohegan Colony had begun to change from the free thinking milieu of my childhood to a more conservative middle class environment. The newly dominant segment of the membership tried hard to dissociate itself from the reputation the founders had earned over the years.

That particular summer, the Robeson Concert organizing committee (which included representatives of neighboring summer communities) was not so politely asked to move the concert out of our community center, where it had been held for several years. We found an open-air facility a few miles away that would be more than adequate – or so we thought.

As the night of the concert approached, rumors began circulating that a demonstration by some local conservative Peekskill organizations, led by veterans groups, would be staged to protest against Paul Robeson's real or purported sympathies toward the Soviet Union.

The fact that this was to be a musical event and nothing else didn't seem to matter. On the day of the concert, as the starting time approached, a small but vociferous crowd began to gather at the entrance gate.

When the demonstrators first began to menace would-be concert-goers, we, the organizing committee, became apprehensive. But when their threats became racist and were followed by overt attacks – beating those who weren't scared off, picking out mixed-race couples or groupings for especially violent treatment – we were shocked. Many were frightened off. But others, including women and children, were already seated and waiting on the concert field. The mob had not yet descended onto the field.

I was dispatched to take our conspicuous old maroon Buick convertible to find a telephone and get the state police to come to our rescue. I was stunned by their response. After serving for three and a half years on active duty in the army,

I had come to think of the authorities as enforcers of law and order. Yet, instead of a few rapid questions to determine what was going on where, followed by them racing to the scene, the response was, "Who's calling? What is your name and address?" and "You know we can't drop everything we're doing to run to stop every street brawl."

When I frantically asked why my biographical details were so important before they could react to such a fearful emergency, I heard snickering on the other end of the line. I realized that we might possibly be better off if they didn't come too soon.

By the time I returned to the scene of the concert, the approach was completely clogged, with cars parked in the middle of the road. I abandoned my car and ran toward the field. With the entrance cut off by the rioting crowd, the only remaining approaches to the area where the stage and seats had been set up was across the open field, through the high grass. But even there, access was blocked.

My heart jumped and began pumping violently when I looked down at the field, through the shadowy figures of these freshly activated vigilantes between me and my friends. There in front of me was a burning cross! The image of the first and only time I had seen a burned cross (as a child, on a camping trip in the very same hills near Peekskill) flashed across my mind.

While I was fruitlessly trying to get the expected help from the authorities, these bullies had descended to the stage and seating area, had made a big stack of all the civil rights literature that was to be for sale at the concert and put a match to it. Not content with this massive book-burning, only four years after the military defeat of world-wide fascism, they had proceeded to torch a crude wooden cross on the field. I slithered through the high grass and joined

Mary and all the others, who were organizing themselves to get to their cars and beat a hasty retreat.

⚜

After what came to be known as The Peekskill Riots, our struggle for human rights took on new meaning and intensity. Though other segments of our population had suffered indignities like these, we students and professionals were personally face to face with politically violent behavior directed against us in our own country for the first time in our lives.

The radical movement, including the left-wing unions, met swiftly to plan our redemptive action. What we came up with was a rescheduled concert at the same site, this time with thousands of concert-goers to be coming up from New York City, including a private volunteer guard recruited primarily from young militant trade unionists to patrol the periphery of the concert field and guard against Klan infiltration.

The whole of New York State was in an uproar, with its bureaucracy under Governor Dewey and the media busily attacking us as radical interlopers, rather than defenders of our constitutional right to freedom of speech and assembly. We saw it as the lines of class struggle being drawn, with most of the conservatives, reactionaries and fascists on one side. On the other side were the radicals, the union workers they influenced, and the more militant believers in civil rights, with some meager support from the shaky liberal front, while the vast majority of the populace remained silent, and apprehensive.

Events had taken control of the second attempt to hold a Robeson Concert out of the hands of our local concert committee, but we fearfully met at our house to plan what role we could play. Our phone ran incessantly with pornographic, racist and anti-Semitic threats on the other end, or at best a receiver slammed in our ears.

We had our car painted blue when one caller threatened to set the "red convertible" afire. An estate in nearby Katonah belonging to personal friends of Paul Robeson had to be guarded around the clock by volunteers until after the concert took place.

The day finally arrived. Well before the scheduled time of the concert, we borrowed a jeep to haul a number of cases of soda to the field where we found a running stream to cool them. Our foresight proved to be very helpful, for there was no drinking water and the young men guarding the periphery of the field all day were able to slake their thirst while trading insults with the hecklers across the road, who had come from all over the state to forcefully register their disapproval.

The concert was uneventful at first: no speeches, only music. But the tension ran so high that it was next to impossible to enjoy the music. When we started to leave the field after the concert was over, the trouble began.

At first the police seemed to do a well-organized job of keeping the demonstrators off the roads so that the departing cars could make their way through the hostile crowds. But then they were seen helping the demonstrators make neat piles of stones, with no noticeable effort to prevent them from being hurled at the departing cars and their helpless occupants.

Since we left in the same open jeep, I picked up a stick, thinking it might be useful if anyone grabbed hold or tried to harass us. As we left the field, the police angrily stopped the jeep to wrest the stick from my hands, admonishing me not to carry a "weapon."

Car windows were smashed, one concert-goer lost the sight of an eye and other extensive damage was inflicted.

Policemen were seen clubbing occupants of the cars, while joining the demonstrators in hurling anti-Semitic and racist epithets. The small radios we carried with us excitedly blasted non-stop, identifying the roads on which the rioters had stationed themselves. Many cars changed their routes as a result. Most of the twenty thousand or so concert-goers made it safely home but only after they snaked their way through the hail of stones thrown by the rioters lining the road in the immediate vicinity of the concert.

There remained the problem of the thousands of guards who were left on the field after all other concert-goers were gone. By this time, many of the unruly protesters had also left, but our guards were without wheels. We decided they would be in a much safer environment if they marched en masse to our community, a few miles away, where we felt they could get rides back home somehow.

They proceeded to do just that, and wound up at our beach-front parking lot, spilling over into the road and onto the beach. Pandemonium broke out among the Mohegan Colony members. Half the community anxiously wrung their hands and couldn't wait until they left, but generally exhibited no overt hostility. They were just afraid of what "the others" might think.

The other half pitched in and started cooking up a storm to feed the hungry young guards. These neighbors sent out an SOS to friends who had cars and drivers who could come and take the young volunteers back to New York City. Even one or two local radio stations helped out by airing an appeal for volunteers.

Mary and I had gone to nearby Yorktown to pick up our son Fred, now two years old. We hadn't dared leave him at our home, which was known and targeted by the hoodlums of the area. Leaving Fred behind, and with pre-natal Nancy accompanying us in utero, we raced back to pitch in, as did many of the concert-goers who had gotten home safely.

They just got right back in their cars and returned to taxi their stranded compatriots back to the safety of their own homes. By three or four o'clock that morning, the parking lot was finally cleared. We felt rightly proud of the Herculean task we had competed with such dispatch, and with absolutely no prior plans or preparations.

⚜

In the aftermath of the concert, the state and even the national officialdom had to answer to the public for its ignominious role. But they stood up to the task valiantly. Statement after statement came from Albany pointing out the general unpopularity of the concert-goers and baldly proclaiming that we had incited the mobs. "Communist groups obviously provoked this incident," said one report. The police were exemplary in performing their task of maintaining order in the face of the "calculated, purposeful incitement of racial conflict," *Life* magazine declared. No mention was made of the breach of the right to public assembly.

There were enough demands from the more informed populace for a public inquiry however, to prod Governor Dewey into appointing an investigative committee. His choice to head up this committee was District Attorney Fanelli of Westchester, who was one of those in charge at the time of the riots, and who had already congratulated the police on having done "a magnificent job." Not surprisingly, Fanelli and his committee concluded that "all police departments that took part in the plan should be commended for their excellent work."

Dewey finally ordered a grand-jury investigation, again to be headed by District Attorney Fanelli. After hearing testimony from several hundred witnesses, the grand jury concluded that the underlying cause of the riots was Robeson's prior inflammatory statements "derogatory to his native land"; that religious and racial hatred was fomented by the Communists; and that the violence "was neither anti-Semitic nor anti-Negro in character."

We locals were left limp – and frightened. I had been under active fire while in the army, but never had I felt hunted and pinpointed for attack. The threatening calls continued for a week or two, and many Peekskill cars sported bumper stickers urging, "Wake up America! Peekskill did!" Most of our local committee members were called before the grand jury to testify – but not Mary and me. They were asked if they had attended meetings in our home, so we were sure that they were saving us for indictments. But somehow the indictments never came.

We moved back to the city shortly thereafter, as we did each fall, in time for school opening, and didn't return until the following spring. The community was still quite nervous. When I walked past our president, a man who I had known intimately from early childhood, the best we could manage was agreement on the need to have helped the guards who had ended up in our area. He certainly didn't condone the violence committed against us, but asked, "Why did you have to bring them here?"

CHAPTER SEVEN

TURBULENCE ON THE HIGH SEAS

"My naive adherence to a system of thought that had actually
inhibited the free independent inquiry I so revered left me
totally unprepared for the shocking Khrushchev revelations."

In the midst of all our hectic neighborhood political activities in the 1950s, a bolt came out of the blue to confound and change the course of my life forever: This was the publication in 1953 of Khrushchev's secret report to the Twentieth Congress of the USSR, revealing the true nature of the Soviet system and the atrocities of the Stalin regime.

In retrospect, it's difficult for me to understand why, until then, I had never seriously questioned my system of beliefs. I had accepted without question a socio-political construct, while thinking that I was analyzing the scene objectively, as a high-minded, unimpeachable intellectual. My naive adherence to a system of thought that had actually inhibited the free independent inquiry I so revered left me totally unprepared for the shocking Khrushchev revelations.

The first informal get-together of a few left-wing friends following Khrushchev's revelations about the horrors of Stalinism proved to be a somber meeting. We were bewildered, confused. We recognized this news as earth-shaking, requiring extensive discussion; but we still hadn't grasped its cataclysmic nature. We had other things on our minds that night: There were electoral politics and there was the need for financial support for our many causes.

But the bubble burst rather quickly. One of our more obstreperous friends asked, "How can we plan to donate one sum or another, when we don't even know which cause we want to support in the first place?" Coming from this hitherto loyal and unquestioning sympathizer, we were shocked out of the inertia that had gripped us. For days afterward, we retired to the quiet of our easy chairs, to read and re-read the report. That was the last time this group convened for political purposes.

The Smith Act trials of the early 1950s – targeting members of the Communist Party – had driven a segment of the leadership underground. I found myself surreptitiously tending to the dental needs of many of them, while at the same time caring for those of Harvey Matusow, the turncoat government witness in the trials. Matusow then made a full 180-degree turn, recanting his testimony and severely damaging the government's case against the second-rung Smith Act victims. These had been confusing times indeed.

Through it all we had staunchly withstood the terrifying onslaught of McCarthyism. Now we discovered that the cause for which we had sacrificed so much had failed us! The McCarthy inquisition had shaken off some of the weaker branches and leaves off the tree, but the ultimate revelations at the Twentieth Congress of the USSR were what poisoned its roots and destroyed the cause for us.

⚜

It was not until years later that I was able to sort out the agony over my own failure to have seen what was happening. We had thought we were analysts and logicians intent upon the path to the truth. The march toward the ultimate goal of "real" freedom for all, particularly the downtrodden masses, was thought of as inexorable.

Then we discovered that dogma had ruled our thinking all along. We faced the eye-opening realization that the "scientific socialism" espoused by Karl Marx was not that scientific. His original concept involved weighing the available facts, coming to a conclusion based on them and then devising optimal methods for achieving social improvement. But to jump from this reasonable sequence to a rigid ideology used to govern all social movement, I ruefully discovered, was the antithesis of scientific objectivity – and, in the wrong hands, had became a justification for a raw seizure of power.

We had castigated Utopian Socialism as unworkable because it was based on faith in human nature and not a realistic, scientifically well-founded analysis of how to achieve a classless society through struggle. Yet, by remaining faithful to the general concepts of so-called scientific socialism, we ended up building a Baal of our own.

It is true that I, and the overwhelming majority of the believers, had no previous knowledge of what went on in the Soviet Union under Stalin. But we should have.

We accepted as facts only that which came from official Soviet sources or from their supporters and rejected any evidence to the contrary as calumny.

It could be characterized more as an ideological betrayal than as simple concealment or distortions of events. But our system of ideas had collapsed. I had built a shell around me that had kept me within the edifice of the cult. Any written or spoken criticism of this carefully built structure was rejected as being willfully destructive.

⚜

Because this discipline of a lifetime of dependence on a restrictive ideology had so inhibited free inquiry, I had to look for totally new ways of thinking; I was groping for a new spiritual center, trying to molt, to shed the axioms, the presumptions upon which I had built my all-encompassing system, in order to make a fresh start.

This re-examination was accompanied by a reawakening of the doubts and uneasiness I had felt in years past about numerous political actions: the Soviet-Nazi Pact, the Soviet invasion of Finland, the Rajk trials in Hungary and Tito's defection, as well as the turn away from Browder's more realistic policy of Twentieth Century Americanism. Very sloppy thinking on my part, I realized, with continual compromise and reluctant acceptance of analyses of these events. I recognized that in a number of cases my doubts had never actually been dispelled, but had merely been suppressed because of my unquestioning acceptance of the principle of so-called democratic centralism.

It wasn't until the Khrushchev volcano erupted that this seemingly orderly process was interrupted. The revelatory lava spilled over the terrain indiscriminately, from top-level functionaries down to the rank and file. Not directly in the line of command, the editorial staff of the *Daily Worker*, their newspaper, took an unprecedented stand and shook the rafters by freely opening its columns to letters to the editor, encouraging independent thought among its readers as well as its own editorial staff.

The ideas spilled out copiously, creating havoc with the previously accepted order of authority. Pandemonium reigned for months, even years, but it became clear that the Party's collapse was inevitable.

Although some Party people never budged, remaining in the same place to this day, it was as though the overwhelming bulk of its membership had boarded the train of change with each getting off at a different station. Some held tightly to what they could salvage. Others tried different station stops along the way. And then there were those who pretty much remained on the train to the other end of the line – and disbelief.

This progressive disillusionment was the most difficult journey I ever experienced. I haven't fully recovered from it to this day. My notes to myself over the years reveal some of my agony, but I don't think I could ever convey the depths of my hurt, disappointment and sense of betrayal.

Through it all, shattering as this discovery proved to be, the motivating force that had driven me to pass my days and years in the pursuit of my lofty goals never was brought into question. But I was set adrift for a decade of searching for some replacement – a way of tying loose ends together to provide myself with a *raison d'être*.

⚜

Thereafter, I attended several sessions of a loose-knit discussion group, consisting of a collection of prominent socialists of all stripes, who gathered together, searching, groping for another way out, but it lasted only a year or so, and didn't coalesce on any alternative. There just wasn't any. They had to settle for a continuation of the wispy goals of peace and freedom, being sought after in already existing broad organizations and in their own individualized concepts of right and wrong.

With my eyes now opened, I could examine the world around me and recognize that democratic control of power was the decisive factor, not the degree to which the wealth of the society was socially or privately owned. The moral or even economic collapse of communism did not mean the victory of capitalism; did not mean capitalist societies wouldn't find it more and more necessary to modify patterns of ownership, as would socialism, to yield some common form of mixed economy.

But without the old guidelines for my life, I was bereft. I had moments of depression and apathy interlaced with the clear and present realization that my life remained a deliciously happy one by anyone's standard, including my own; that I had what I have always revered: a wonderful family, friends, health and circumstances that permitted me to enjoy all of these in relative comfort. And with a strong sense of conscience still intact.

The self-righteous certainty of my youth was no longer there; only rootlessness in its stead. My community activities went on, for I felt that therein lay the continuity of my vaunted values and past goals. The hunt went on for some system of thought that could join these to the social orientation of an activist, of someone whose personal validity and sense of self-worth was tied to his relationship with society overall.

I found no such system, but somehow managed to place the ensuing restlessness on the back burner of my otherwise fulfilled life. My family was blossoming in a perpetual spring. The pleasure of uninterrupted exuberant growth engulfed me. We skied, played tennis and swam; we introduced our children to books, concerts, ballets and plays; and when they reached an appropriate age, we traveled together.

CHAPTER EIGHT

UNDER SAIL AGAIN

"How ever did a Brooklyn-born Jewish dentist find himself so totally absorbed by and immersed in the African continent?"

Mary's romantic and unquenchable thirst for excitement, adventure and travel made its first major breakthrough in 1959, three years after the Khrushchev revelation. Strange that we use an event so far removed from us geographically and personally as such a consequential landmark, but that had represented a real turning point for us. Our perceived responsibilities to society at large prior to that had been such that we had so interwoven our family, political, and professional lives that we had little spare time for such trivial pursuits as travel for pleasure.

But Mary had a voracious appetite, an uncanny ability to work out the details no matter how insurmountable they seemed at first glance, and an adventurous soul. Our political agenda no longer weighed quite so heavily. Somehow the world would not fall apart if we didn't attend that meeting or demonstration. Though we were still active, the sense of urgency was now behind us.

By 1959, Nancy was nine, Fred twelve – old enough for overseas travel, we thought. But I was dragging my tail. "What will be left of my practice when I return? Will we be able to finance our travels?" All the straw people I could set up, all the obstacles I could raise, were methodically knocked down by my spouse – one by one. We would borrow the money if it wasn't available at departure time. We would go with another family – Janine and Sol, friends with two children the same age as ours – rent a car in Europe, stop at very modestly priced pensions.

Mary had by this time severed her professional ties to the Hammer Brothers (Armand of Occidental Petroleum fame and Victor, Director of the Hearst Art Collection at Gimbel's Department Store). She was then in business for herself as an interior designer. The plan that Mary created was ambitious. She and Janine would travel together two months. When school was out, Sol and I would follow with the children. We would spend two summer months traveling all together through France, Italy and Yugoslavia. Sol and I would then return, leaving the children with the wives for another two months.

Each in our turn, we crossed the Atlantic by ocean liner. The heroic husbands and accompanying children were met in Paris by two delighted ladies who just couldn't contain their glee at having spent two glorious, footloose months in France and Spain. Needless to say, my own travels turned out to be just as glorious. Regretfully, my first great vacation spree ended after two months, when I deposited the women and children in a small rented villa at Lido di Lavinia on the Mediterranean shore, a short distance from La Bella Roma.

Back home childless and wifeless, I was a drifter for two months, going from one relative to another, one friend to another. I hadn't been alone like that for fifteen years – since my return from the war – and I felt abandoned. Despite my concerns, my practice was not only intact, but had actually grown in my absence. An associate had been developing his own practice while helping me with my overflow, and my nurse and friend of many years standing had seen to it that old patients stuck and new patients waited for me, while emergencies were handled on the spot.

⁂

There were lessons learned: First, that I need not worry about my practice and that I could feel free to take relatively long holidays without undue concern. Second, that warnings to Mary about building her dream house too high because her concept of travel was so foolishly romantic were, in fact, foolishly groundless. And, third, that I would never voluntarily stay at home while wife and children were meandering around the globe. The world would be my oyster too.

For the next few summers we traipsed around Eastern and Western Europe, including the Balkans and the USSR. There we searched high and low for some signs of the "Socialist Man," but found that Muscovites pushed and shoved to get on a crowded street car just as vigorously as did New Yorkers getting on and off the IRT.

We went to Egypt and couldn't believe that upon our arrival in Cairo at dawn, there, stretched beneath the window of our Nile Hilton Hotel room was the ancient Nile itself, with its other-world atmosphere of packets, tugboats, and cargo ships along with a myriad of small vessels with twinkling lights that gradually disappeared as the sun poked its leading edge over the horizon. There below us was all the romance this poor unemotional soul and devotee of the world of ideas could muster up.

Then in short order came the Sphinx and Pyramids, with native Egyptian friends there to skillfully guide us through the thousands of years of history that passed by. I was at last emerging from the depression that had settled over me during the preceding years of political disillusionment.

⁕

These few years of adventure and travel found me scratching the periodic itch for involvement that had begun to gnaw at me, but still with no resolution in view. While the signs were not evident to me at the time, this was about to change.

Just one year after the start of this era of extensive travel, in 1960, we were invited by African-American friends of ours to a cocktail-tea reception they were giving in their suburban home at the request of the State Department, to welcome to the U.N. the foreign minister from the newly liberated nation of Nigeria and his delegation. There, at the tail end of the reception line was a Nigerian gentlemen in native garb, short in stature and short in neck, almost turtle-like, who greeted our family, and especially thirteen-year-old Fred, a bit more warmly than did his fellow delegates. That was Aminu Kano.

We lingered while Fred eagerly threw simple questions about life in Nigeria at him and drew relatively simple but thoughtful responses. Before we knew it, Fred had screwed up enough courage to ask him if he would consider addressing an assembly of his student body – this without even consulting the school authorities. The disarming informal response was, "Sure. Just tell me when." A week or so later we were picking him up at his hotel to deliver him to Fred's school for his talk to the students!

Mary Feinstein, George Weissman, Perry Miller Adato, 1983

With Brock Peters, Martin Luther King, Dede Peters, Norman Eisner
and friend, 1964

Thus began a long and fast friendship covering many continents and circumstances. The meeting also set the scene for a major re-routing in my life; one that would take me out of my doldrums, stop my drift and put me on course once again. It was this same Mallam Aminu Kano who proved to be the principal catalyst for change in his own country.

Each succeeding year Mallam Aminu returned for a two – or three – month stint as a delegate to the U.N. When he wanted to escape the succession of formal meetings by day and the innumerable and interminable diplomatic receptions by night, he retreated to the informality of our home, family and friends.

⚜

By the fall of 1962, we were ready to embark on our most ambitious trip by far: We were going around the world. While discussing our plans with Aminu he interjected, "Well, why don't you return from Asia via Africa? I'll give you introductory letters to a few people along the route." This sounded exciting and possible, and that's the way it went.

Our orbit started with a trans-continental crossing to San Francisco and Los Angeles, notable for our visit to Disneyland. Notable, that is, for the many slides Fred took of the make-believe animals on the African boat ride. We mingled them with all our other slides taken later on a real safari in East Africa, and dared any poor victims we subsequently could lure into our living room to view our slide show to distinguish between the real thing and the Disney version.

Then on to the Far East – Japan, Hong Kong, Singapore, Thailand, Burma, Vietnam, Pakistan and India. The travel agent had put together a remarkably inexpensive ticket, which he said was the longest he had ever written. We had prepared our trip reasonably well in other respects.

In addition to Aminu's letters of introduction to heads of state, cabinet members and other dignitaries of the African states we were to visit, both Mary and I had done a job with Asia. Here was a Japanese-American friend whose parents were in Tokyo, an Indian friend, and a Canadian at the World Bank who had gone to school with several leaders of Asian states. There were patients and friends who had contacts in countries we were to visit. We filed away every name given to us, and used them as we were able. We even excitedly exchanged names and addresses with a fellow passenger in a Manhattan elevator, when we overheard him describing his home in Nairobi. We, of course, ended up visiting him there.

Our first visit to Kenya and Tanzania centered around the wild animals of the game preserves. But these two countries were also the first occasion we had to take advantage of the letters of introduction Aminu had given us. In Kenya we spoke to Tom Mboya's wife; he was out of the country at the time. Joseph Murumbi, the vice-president of the nation graciously met with me. I interviewed several cabinet members in Tanzania, but the pinnacle of our visit came when the whole family met with Julius Nyerere, who was then president of Tanzania.

When we presented Aminu's letter, Nyerere proved to be as warm and friendly and hospitable as Aminu himself. Fred, our family photographer, had to take pictures of the family posing with him and his Hawaiian shirt and stockinged feet (his shoes had been kicked off under his desk), but suddenly realized that he had only one or two frames left on the roll. Flustered, in his excitement, he started to open the camera, exposing the film briefly, eventually leaving us with only one photo of the President, and that slightly streaked. Mwalimu (teacher), the designation he preferred as his honorary title, laughed and joked with us over the incident.

Party at Armand Hammer's estate, with Julius Hammer and Mary

At same party, Victor and Armand Hammer, and Fred Gimbel

With Pauline Nadler, Fortune Goldenbaum, Fred Nadler, Joe Goldenbaum and Mary, Alexandra, Egypt, 1959

We compared notes on the U.S.A. and his country, and he gave us a note to deliver to Aminu. Although Aminu was the primary motivating factor in turning my attention to the African continent, our contact with Julius Nyerere surely abetted the process.

From Tanzania we crossed the continent via Khartoum, to West Africa and Nigeria. Aminu Kano greeted us at the Lagos airport and had his driver take us to the house which served as our residence for the duration of our stay in Lagos, as guests of the government. He had told the prime minister, Abubaker Tafawa Balewa, of our importance to him on his annual trips as a delegate to the U.N. and consequently the prime minister provided us with quarters. The disclosure that just prior to our stay the same house had been occupied by Obafemi Awolowo, the leader of the Western Region opposition party before he was jailed on charges of plotting against the government, wasn't exactly settling, but it was exciting.

We did the usual tourist rounds, looked at Lagos' modern buildings, the museum, parliament, and the harbor. But the high point was a visit to a suburb of Lagos to attend a political rally with Aminu. The clenched-fist salute of his followers, we later learned, was an old Hausa sign of greeting, symbolizing the spilling of the good earth, and predating its use by the Third International by a century or more. We continued through West Africa, stopping in Ghana, Liberia, Ivory Coast, Senegal, Guinea and Morocco before we finally left the continent for home.

Everything about that trip fired my blood. This wasn't vacation travel. A whole new world had opened up to me. I was not born for the depressing cynicism that had been creeping up on me for close to a decade. My love affair with Africa had aroused again enthusiasm in me. I became consumed with the thought that intensive concentration and study of Africa, its history and politics, could ultimately lead me to a productive and fulfilling continuity for my life.

᯽

Some decades later, when I began to think in terms of converting my occasional jottings over the years into a more organized form, it was this phase of my life – my time as an African scholar – that intrigued me most.

How ever did a Brooklyn-born Jewish dentist find himself so totally absorbed by and immersed in the African continent, with almost all of his extracurricular time and even extensive curricular time devoted to it? When the political urgency was no longer at white-heat and travel was still a seasonal diversion, how did I end up the chronicler of one of Nigeria's heroes?

What happens in the present is always built on one's past. I felt my whole life provided the context for this turn of events. During those earlier years, just like my apparent patron saint Don Quixote before me, it had never really occurred to me that there was an alternative other than immediate response to the injustices around me. I had just assumed it was my personal responsibility to try to right any wrong.

But when, with Khruhschev's revelations of the mid 1950's, all my previous assumptions were placed in question, a deep political lethargy had come over me. It wasn't until many years had passed that my lethargy evolved into a kind of disengagement that permitted me to sit back and assure myself that whatever my personal actions, they were not likely to alter the world significantly in the near or distant future.

I had reasoned that I could continue within limits to contribute financially to an obviously worthy cause and fall back on my age as an excuse for my lack of more active involvement. I had slowly molted and emerged a checkbook liberal. Along with this change in my responses to the world around me, I apparently found a renewed, perhaps more diffuse, but greatly expanded and more flexible, sense of right and wrong. I no longer saw life in stark contrasts, nor was I so sure of my allies or foes.

It was my association with Aminu Kano that focused and renewed my faith in people, even including some who were at or near the top. It was to me a new and more mature faith that I had found, tempered by a pragmatism somewhat freer of dogma and illusion. I no longer could be sure of anything, but this unassuming man seemed a refreshing political breeze blowing through the developing world.

CHAPTER NINE

A NEW PORT OF CALL

"I began to think that my new-found love for the continent of Africa could result in a written work ..."

The first rumblings of a need to put my random thoughts down on paper began to emerge during my school years. At the time, the recording of scattered notes was basically for my own edification. Although I had held onto these notes tenaciously and had even been editor of our student newspaper, it had not occurred to me to try to organize my writing endeavors into story or essay form until I was whiling away all that spare time available to me while in the army, in the customary military fashion of "hurry up and wait."

During that time I became an habitual writer of journal entries and managed to produce a few essays. The bulk of my observations, however, took the form of long rambling letters to friends and family, a practice that was eventually dominated by my daily love letters to Mary during almost a year of courtship followed by another year of imposed marital separation while I served in the European Theater of Operations.

It wasn't until two decades later, during the "Africa" years of the 1960s, that resort to writing again became my refuge. With those early experiences with scattered short-story, diary writing and notes to myself as a launching pad, I began to think that my penchant for expressing myself in writing, combined with my new-found love for the continent of Africa could produce a written work that could be my contribution to society.

⚜

Although my contact with Nigeria intrigued me, in the beginning a focus on Julius Nyerere and Tanzania seemed more alluring. Here was a socialist country with leaders trying to mold a nation according to new rules, rethinking and refitting the autocracy encouraged by the international Communist world.

This country was going to forge its way upward toward development through a truly peoples' government. There would be free elections, and popular control using what came to be known as Ujamaa (Village) Socialism: A path that seemed to me at the time to be the paradigm I had been groping for.

On our first trip to Africa I had met Jane Wicken, Nyerere's personal and political secretary, and several cabinet members as well as the president himself. One year and dozens of books, newspapers and periodicals later, the idea struck me that an initial, though formidable, start for my writing career could be a biography of Mwalimu Julius himself.

or need for pomp. When a series of letters to Nyerere and the several people around him whom I had met finally elicited a response, it was a disappointing one. President Nyerere sent warm personal regards and appreciation for my interest in him and his country, but he felt that he wasn't ready at that stage to take the time out for the cooperation I was requesting. And, in any case, if and when he reached the point when he felt that a biography should be written, I surely could understand that he would want a fellow Tanzanian to do it. But, he went on, why don't I consider writing a biography of his country?

⚜

It took me a while to get over my initial disappointment, but then his suggestion began to intrigue me. Had there ever been such an undertaking? How would it be different from a history of a nation, or even a travel book?

So there I was, looking for the answers to these questions by using the next available stretch of time, the summer of 1965, to investigate the possibility of such a project. As preparation, I had been poring over any books or articles I could lay my hands on that would provide me with the needed background material. I hosted and drove the Tanzanian Minister Swai to Princeton University when he came to New York to address a conference there, and of course pumped him for any information that might be helpful.

Upon my return to Dar Es Salaam, Jane Wicken laid out plans for me to interview several cabinet members as well as herself, but suggested that the president was deeply involved in affairs of state and wouldn't be nearly as accessible to me as on our previous visit some two years ago. And she arranged for a flight to visit Zanzibar, the fabled island just off the coast of Tanganyika (so-called before Zanzibar was joined to it to form its newer incarnation, Tanzania), where we would be received by a member of the island's politbureau, Aboud Jumbe.

That visit to Zanzibar, the Spice Island, is remembered almost as whimsy. Our host remained with us from the time he picked us up at the airport to the time he waved goodbye at the same airport, with the sunset behind him as backdrop, and with the strong odor of clove permeating the atmosphere, providing a fitting reminder of all its history of Arab dominance, slave markets and the island's role as one of the primary sources of cloves for the world.

A running discussion for the entire time we were together culminated in what was tantamount to an ad hoc meeting of several members of the polit bureau, not too different from what I pictured as a similar committee meeting back in New York. The stale Marxist jargon had a much too familiar ring. Queries about reputed massacres of Arabs, or at the very least, breaches of human rights, were brushed aside with talk of how long the Arabs had exploited the island's native population. But our host did sound bright and informed, and apparently wielded much influence in the government of the island.

Flying back from Zanzibar to the mainland, we were dismayed by the familiar pattern, and wondered if and how the newly merged nation of Tanzania could check this semi-autonomous and recently acquired tail from wagging the dog. How could this independent nation make the grade, while having to deal with the kind of rigid thinking that dominated that small island?

It was not surprising when upon the assassination of Zanzibar's chief of state several years later, our friend and guide was chosen to head its government. I should note that there was some moderation of policy when he took over.

Evidently "democratic centralism" had held him in check until he emerged as Mr. Centralism himself, and could adopt a decision-making role.

⚜

At that juncture, my wearisome life-long association with powerless groups fighting losing battles from the outside, notwithstanding what I understood to be the moral superiority of their ideas, had predisposed me to turn my attention to Tanzania. In Tanzania a popular progressive leader and the movement he led were in a controlling position, able to move decisively to put their principles to work.

As it would turn out, their ideas for their nation were not any more effective or successful in the long run than their very much larger counter-part, the former Soviet Union, despite the many differences between them. Although Tanzania maintained a one-party system, rather than a multi-party democracy, its leaders never resorted to the gross excesses of the Communist world. Nevertheless, such a restrictive policy helped them little to overcome their position as one of the poorest nations on earth.

Upon our return to mainland Tanzania, I followed up with further personal in-depth interviews with government officials and visits to several villages in the hinterlands before we returned to New York City. It was then that I realized the work I was considering was not really of much value or interest. But while bemoaning the impending aborting of my project, it suddenly struck me that Aminu was the man I should have been concentrating on all along.

CHAPTER TEN

AMINU KANO

"Aminu Kano appeared to me as a sort of alter ego."

Mallam Aminu Kano. Although my own philosophical underpinnings had long seemed in a state of disarray, this unassuming man appeared as a refreshing political breeze blowing through the newly developing third world nations. His example roused an enthusiasm in me that I had not felt for many years.

As I read whatever I could find about his work and talked to anyone I could find who knew him on any level, the more I learned about him, his attitudes, his hopes and desires, and his role in the independence struggle, the closer I felt to him. My interest in Aminu personalized my avid interest in Africa.

He appeared to me as a sort of alter ego. Background? Totally different from mine. Religion? Race? Nationality? Class? Geography? Nowhere near Manhattan, U.S.A. Aminu lived and thought and spoke as I pictured I should and would, were I in his shoes.

I wrote an article, *"The Dilemma of Power,"* as though I were faced with his problems myself. My cynicism about politicians and their motivations began to weaken. Could there be an honest and dedicated politician in this world, one who stood within striking distance of a power center?

Nigeria at the time was already locked in the throes of a debilitating political struggle among its three regions – North, East and West – each dominated by a major ethnic group. Aminu's party, the NEPU (Northern Elements Progressive Union), a minority anti-authoritarian party based in the predominantly Muslim and Hausa-speaking Northern Region, was attempting to bridge the ethnic divide by an alliance with the NCNC (National Conference of Nigerian Citizens). The NCNC base was in the Yoruba-speaking South, but was strongest among the Ibos of the Eastern Region.

My past challenges seemed to have been cut out of similar cloth. I realized that it was my own background and attitudes that lured me toward a new, yet familiar, battle. I had grown up believing that "all men are created equal," and this general conviction and its derived understanding of fairness over the years had become an inherent part of me.

⁂

The more I thought about it and the deeper I delved into the political and personal history of Aminu Kano, the more I realized that concentrating on him and his relationship with his country was the right choice.

Although Aminu was not yet the leader of his nation, it struck me that I might be able to explore the reasons why so many millions of Africans believed and trusted in him and thus convey what I learned to a significant number of readers.

I believed that a thoughtful biography of Aminu Kano could make a recognizable contribution to a broad audience in my native U.S.A. as well as in Nigeria and Africa.

I was not likely to find another prominent subject so close to my own heart and conscience as Aminu. This consideration was crucial, for in the course of the soul-searching that comes with a sincere attempt at relatively objective research, I would have found it extremely difficult to write anything I didn't believe completely.

At this time I was also reexamining my ideas about the relationship of the masses to their leaders in the political process. During my Marxist days, I had accepted the Plekhanov analysis that leadership would rise from the ranks when the interplay of mass forces called for it.

But my proximity to the political leadership in Africa was giving me a new perspective: Hard work, dedication and keen perception of the forces one wanted to lead could enable an individual to build a movement around himself, to gain a position of leadership without necessarily being nurtured by a logical progression or a chain of command. A man or woman in such a position could exert an independent force on the course of history.

I saw Franklin Delano Roosevelt as such a leader. His record as a mildly moderate politician when he first became president of the United States in no way qualified him for, nor prepared the country for, the militant role he eventually played. No movement existed from which he could have arisen. After assuming office he saw the nation as damaged, needing emergency repair. The reality of the depression had to be faced. He took firm action to combat it – action never before taken. He was never part of a movement of the masses that thrust him into the presidency. He didn't represent them. He led them.

I saw Aminu in the same light. His was a patrician's background, though he started his career as a teacher because in Nigeria at the time there were few other alternatives open for him. He organized the first independent people's association in Northern Nigeria, a teacher's union, and led them through some basic struggles for improving conditions for themselves and the students under them. This served to launch him as a leader of people – a politician.

Though the choice was his to speak for the *talakawa* (common person), not vice versa, millions of the conservative, traditional, deeply religious northern masses and young exuberant students and intellectuals flocked to his banner. He too was in advance of the people he led, and moved them in a direction none of them had planned or anticipated, yet never found himself so far ahead that he lost contact with them – the quality of true leadership. He, his ideas and his approach seemed to reflect my own as they had evolved from my association with would-be martyrs and heroes who once thought they would save the world from itself. And my own role, I hoped, would be to record the process.

I wasn't looking solely for a subject to launch my literary career. I was also searching for an outlet for my newly reorganized political agenda, and I couldn't conjure up an image of anyone coming closer to representing this agenda than Aminu. Except that unlike me, he was in a position to do something about it.

In addition, if my efforts were ever to be published, it could conceivably help further Aminu's career, while reinforcing this mutual political stance. Yes, and this could certainly have a much more tangible effect on world events than I had been able to produce up until then. But I wasn't up to worrying about getting a book published yet.

The challenge at that point was to get a book written. The

coalescing of all these political and literary goals of mine, and the real probability that they might be significantly advanced by a project such as this, created an almost uncontrollable surge of excitement in me. The only major hurdle I faced was the needed cooperation of Mallam Aminu.

꧁꧂

It was the fall of 1965, and Nigeria was convulsed with political crises, one after the other. The elections of December 1964 had been a total mess. In the months before the election, the political parties had divided down the middle with Aminu's party, the Northern Elements Progressive Union (NEPU), aligning itself with the UPGA (United Progressive Grand Alliance) against the ruling NPC (Northern Peoples' Congress) and a scattering of minor allies.

Seeing no clear victory in sight, the UPGA decided to boycott the national election. The results were mixed. Where UPGA parties were in control of local governments, the whole electoral process was shut down. In the North where Aminu's opponents held local sway, the boycott was put into effect but the polls remained open, leading to an obviously distorted result.

The chaos that followed, eventually resulted in a "compromise." New elections were held only in those areas where the polling booths had actually remained closed. That solution, of course, left the Northern Region where Aminu and his party NEPU were predominant, completely excluded from the political process.

Although Aminu's overwhelming popularity in key sections in the nation, particularly in the Kano Emirate area, was unquestioned, when his followers abstained from voting he found himself outside the pale. The turmoil continued into

1965 when the Western Region elections were held. These, in turn, were so obviously rigged that virtual civil war resulted.

Fortuitously, Aminu appeared once again at the U.N. in New York, in December of that year. At that point I was able to propose my project to him. After some initial modest reluctance, he agreed to cooperate. He left his prayer rug and some luggage at our home, fully expecting to return as a delegate to an economic conference two or three weeks later. But it was a full three years before he returned. The first military coup exploded on January 15, 1966, less than three weeks after Aminu returned to Nigeria, and Nigerian politics had been turned on its head.

Many of his followers were elated at this turn of events, for they had been excluded and completely disenfranchised by the previous regime. But Aminu remained wary of the new military leadership. Though his core constituency was in the North, he had always maintained good working relationships with southerners, and particularly the Ibos both those in their home area in the Eastern Region as well as those who had migrated to the North as trades-people and civil servants.

Yet General Aguiyi-Ironsi, the new head of state, despite his attempt to weld together a unified state, impressed Aminu and many other northerners as inept and Ibo-oriented. Aminu wanted to wait and see. The more impulsive and less astute of Aminu's followers who rushed to endorse the new regime ultimately were proven wrong, and several ended up in jail.

The mostly Ibo coup-makers had killed off the discredited, predominantly northern political and military leaders who had dominated the national scene until then, and although the coup had been partially aborted, what emerged was a new set of military leaders who knew little about political give and take.

The logical person for the military rulers to have turned to for support in the predominantly Muslim North was the leader of the opposition, namely Aminu. With the old leadership either assassinated or running for cover, he was the only major figure who had emerged from the coup and all these crises untainted by the displaced regime and with enough status and courage to retain the confidence of northerners, rich and poor.

The military was in office but three or four months when northern Hausa-Fulanis, distrustful of the regime and fearful of being dominated by the Ibos, exploded in devastating riots throughout the Northern Region, resulting in the deaths of many Ibos and flight southward to Ibo land for many of those who had lived in the North up to then. It was a tough period for Aminu. He was the northern Nigerian leader most associated with maintaining a good working relationship with Ibos, and at the time distrust between the two groups was at its emotional peak.

With no significant allies in the more populous North, and with northerners dominating the lower ranks of the army, Ironsi's regime was overthrown, lasting only six months. A seemingly more neutral figure, Colonel Yakubu Gowon, a Christian from a small ethnic group in the North, was installed as the new supreme commander. Colonel (now General) Gowon did turn to Aminu, asking him to join his cabinet as commissioner of communications, and later as commissioner of health.

He also prevailed upon Aminu and three others to use their influence in the troubled North to help convince any doubters of the urgent need to build a national consensus, a One Nigeria, rather than to follow the impulse to split the country into several independent nations.

Although General Gowon tried to involve all regional and

ethnic groups in his government, unfortunately tragic riots in the North, inflicted by predominantly Muslim Hausa-Fulanis against resident Ibos, led to many deaths both before and after he took over. These left the country sharply divided. Within a year the protracted Biafran Rebellion broke out, lasting almost three years, with the Ibos warring against the rest of the country in an unsuccessful attempt at secession.

Without attempting to predict what role Aminu would play in his country's future – without even knowing whether his leadership would survive these violent upheavals – I came to the realization that he had already had a deep, long-lasting effect on his people.

CHAPTER ELEVEN

A BOOK IS BORN

"Those months of research in Nigeria were a major turning point in my life. My attention to local and national politics here in the U.S. was pushed aside. Now writing and Nigeria became all-important."

During this period of turmoil in Nigeria and in Aminu's life my own *chef d'oeuvre* was gestating. Back in New York City I was busy accumulating facts, stories and background material as I befriended members of Nigeria's diplomatic community in New York, centered around the United Nations, as well as Nigerian academics and American Africanists specializing in Nigerian affairs.

My son Fred, then a student at Swarthmore College, once again arranged to have Aminu address a student group on one of his visits to New York. One of Fred's professors introduced me to academicians at nearby Haverford and at

Northwestern University in Illinois, who were involved in one way or another with Nigeria. Following these leads, I spent a long weekend at Northwestern, where I used its extensive African Studies Department and met with Professor John Paden, who had recently completed his doctoral thesis on the interweaving of religion and political culture in Kano, Nigeria.

The Northwestern visit was followed by a day trip to Stony Brook and several visits to Princeton, where I met with the head of their Black Studies Department, Dr. C.S. Whitaker. Dr. Whitaker had written his doctoral thesis, "The Politics of Tradition," on the interrelationship of politics and traditional leadership in Northern Nigeria during an era of change and modernization, as well as a brilliant article on the relationship between the three prominent leaders of the North: the Sardauna of Sokoto, premier of the Northern Region; the prime minister of Nigeria, Abubakar Tafawa Balewa; and Aminu. The two, other than Aminu in this triumvirate, were ultimately assassinated in the coup as leaders of the displaced regime. Aminu as leader of the opposition survived.

I found an amazing receptivity among these professional Africanists, with only a slight reserve from some quarters over the presumptuousness of an intruder, a dentist of all things. But the dominant response was unreservedly warm and cooperative. In my future dealings with this group of scholars, their complete acceptance continued, though on occasion it might have been accompanied by a slight shaking of the head in awe of my persistence.

These contacts proved to be a gold mine of background information and insights for me, preparing me for my next sojourn in Nigeria, during the summer of 1969 – a three-month stint of library research and extensive interviews with Aminu and those who had been part of his life.

✦

Initial interviews with Aminu in Lagos and Kano evolved into many hours of taped conversations probing the events and attitudes in his personal life; his background culture and relationships with the people around him; and far-ranging discussions about his politics, philosophy, goals and tactics. Out of these hours of dialogue came a long list of people to interview throughout the country – family, friends and political associates.

My special relationship with Aminu, coupled with my apparent status as a western intellectual, opened the doors wide for me. Almost everyone I met or interviewed spoke freely about his or her life and how it intersected with Aminu's, holding back none of their memories or impressions save when the format of my interview unwittingly intruded upon their traditions. Though unfamiliar with this unexpected reluctance, I soon realized that the distance between me and the Nigerians interviewed was far more than geographic in nature.

I had to depend heavily on these often devious, contradictory or repetitious interviews, for much of Nigeria's record keeping was in oral form, and what I could find in personal or library files was frequently limited, without proper indexing. But what gave me the most difficulty were the customs of the region. A library knowledge of Hausa-Fulani customs had given me some understanding and made me more aware of the cultural differences, but this hardly lessened my difficulties.

The traditional extended family relationships and taboos, partly in the process of change, were perplexing to me, an American, for it wasn't easy to sort the new from the traditional. I spent one whole afternoon interviewing and extracting the intimate details of her life from a woman introduced to me as Aminu's sister, only to discover subsequently that she was no more than a distant relative of his according to our Western rigid categories of family.

Kano market, 1979

Interviewing Nigerians for Aminu Kano's biography, 1970

Kano family compound,
1980

Interviewing Aminu Kano's relatives in the compound
where the African leader was born.

Kano market
street scene,
1980

Information that I had assumed would be readily available took many additional hours to unravel when the interviewee had to circumvent a question, or answer it deviously because of the "avoidance patterns," or societal limitations on who could be mentioned or how one could refer to a relative.

Even my interpreter wasn't able to help too much in this regard, for try as he might, he too was deeply interwoven in the web of tradition I was trying to penetrate. For example, a mother could never speak directly to her son, and once he reached his teens could not even refer to him by his first name; they communicated only through intermediaries. It was worth noting that even the people I met who had been educated in the west found it difficult to explain these differences and restrictions, the customs were so integral a part of their growing up.

These personal and cultural aspects of my investigations particularly interested Mary when she finally arrived. She identified with the women and loved to delve into the intricate patterns of intermarriage and polygamy, of the effect of purdah, the cultural practice of restricting a Muslim wife (up to four per household) to her quarters, not to be seen by any man other than her husband without his explicit permission, and the custom wherein the first-born (and frequently other children as well) was given to substitute parents, usually respected, well-placed relatives or friends.

Once she was on the scene, Mary put her considerable organizing skills to work, making the necessary contacts and preparing for my interviews, transport, and so forth. It was a well-functioning, reasonably well-oiled team, even though we didn't always see eye to eye on approach and methodology.

❧

Those three months of research in Nigeria were a major turning point in my life. My attention to local and national politics here in the U.S. was pushed aside. Now writing and Nigeria became all-important. Our long and numerous vacations became Africa-oriented with Nigeria as the core, although we did try to stop in other African and European countries en route each time.

Basically, my profession changed. My dental chair time was cut to four days and eventually only three days per week. This, of course, also cut down on family income, but I can't recall Mary ever complaining or suggesting that I put in more work time. She just continued with her interior design work, and we managed reasonably well.

I don't know how she did it, but she was also able to fend off enough of the social distractions, responsibilities and chores that are part of most middle class lives to permit me to devote the overwhelming bulk of my time out of the office to writing and research. Paradoxically, I somehow was able to get more done during those first few years than I am able to accomplish now, after my retirement from dentistry. My ability to concentrate and intense motivations were at their peak, no doubt.

I would submerge myself in Africa each evening after a day of dentistry, a quick dinner, and a briefing on the family's activity that day. I was at my desk a couple of hours each evening and daytime hours on my weekdays or weekends off. It should have been a grueling time of my life, but is not at all remembered that way. My renewed vision of a productive life had re-energized me.

⚜

After a few chapters were written in rough draft, there had to be some kind of affirmation – interest on the part of a publisher. I examined the books most recently acquired for my

Africana library and hit upon Cambridge University Press, a prestigious label that had already published on Africa and that should have some idea of the role Aminu Kano was playing in Nigeria.

I let my fingers do the walking through the Yellow Pages, made the required phone calls and managed to wangle an appointment with their senior editor in New York City, David Winsor, my first contact with a publisher. To my surprise, he was interested and agreed to read the couple of chapters I had on hand. My surprise turned to elation when he said he liked what I had written to that point, and though he couldn't guarantee anything, he felt that if I continued in the same vein he certainly would submit the completed manuscript to the London office with a favorable recommendation to the publication committee.

I could hardly believe my ears! The very first submission with such a positive response. All I had heard before had prepared me for multiple rejections and a harrowing search for a publisher. I did feel I had prepared the groundwork carefully and had hoped for, but never really expected, such smooth sailing.

My self-confidence soared, sending me back to my desk and a greatly intensified pace, even feverish. As I finished another chapter or two I would submit them, receive procedural suggestions and glow at the accompanying favorable comments. A personal relationship with David Winsor, my editorial consultant, developed in the process and everything was rolling along smoothly.

By 1971, the manuscript was completed. I had submitted the final text to Aminu to check the accuracy of the facts contained within, but he returned it to me untouched and obviously pleased with the result. Then a disastrous setback occurred. Winsor had decided to leave the firm. He kept his

promise to me and got his successor to submit the manuscript to the publishing committee in England, but with no
senior editor to push for acceptance it was eventually turned
down. Assurances all round me that this happened all the
time did not assuage my disappointment.

I realized that if I had not initially had such a positive
response from such a prestigious publishing house, it would
have been a great deal more difficult to muster up the energy
and spirit needed to complete the book, but I was crest-fallen
nevertheless. Such uninterrupted momentum to that point,
yet there I was, back at square one, facing the Herculean task
of circulating my manuscript. But I couldn't take any time
out for a let-down. Depression would most certainly take over
and my self-esteem would plummet if I did.

When presented with my manuscript, each publishing
house that agreed to read it would, according to custom,
assume it had an exclusive while the book was being considered. But that would stretch the process interminably while I
awaited the expected rejection. So I photocopied four or five
copies of the completed manuscript and handed them to any
publisher who would seriously consider the book. It was a
risky enterprise.

I was surprised to find that almost everyone I
approached considered my project serious enough to read
through the manuscript, and not reject it out of hand. I did
choose carefully, looking for a referral from anyone who
knew a publisher. Three of the four who read it kept it for
further consideration by those who made the ultimate decision.

Grosset & Dunlop at the time had an Africa list headed by
a Nigerian who liked the work and was ready to go. He submitted the manuscript three or four times in rapid succession
to the publishing committee, but each time it was postponed
for later consideration. It was still going through this process

Nancy, Julius Nyerere (then President of Tanzania), and Mary, 1963

Ambassador Godow, Mary and Ms. Portia Ogbu and husband
at their wedding

when I gladly withdrew it. Quadrangle/New York Times Publishers, which had also been considering the book, had accepted it and offered me a contract. I was crazy with joy and agreed to any terms they offered.

The mechanics of getting a manuscript published were set in motion: check the editor's corrections, accept or reject them, read line proofs, page proofs, index, choose photos, etc. None of which fazed me one bit. The hard part was over. It was euphoria and I was on Cloud Nine. My book was being published.

One of the selling points that had convinced Quadrangle/ New York Times to offer a contract was that I had already been approached by a British publisher who wanted to buy the rights for sale and distribution in Nigeria. That sale alone, what with my minimal advance, cut their investment down and would enable them to cover their expenses with little effort. But that was good news as well as bad. I naively had assumed that if they agreed to publication they would push hard for publicity in an effort to make a profit.

To my dismay, the 10 percent of the cost of publication that is ordinarily allotted to promotion and advertising was not forthcoming. Their concept of publishing was evidently to put out a number of modest titles and hope that one or more of them would take off on its own. If that occurred, then they would start pumping promotional capital into it. They even protested when we tried to initiate our own promotion, maintaining that it would interfere with their other titles.

With those limitations, needless to say, my book, *African Revolutionary: Life and Times of Nigeria's Aminu Kano*, did not take off here in the U.S., although it did have a different reception in Nigeria. Aminu was known in every corner of the country and interest was high. Distribution of the book by Aminu's adherents was also politically expedient, and it was pushed accordingly.

But all of that was of little financial value to the American publisher, for they had sold the Commonwealth rights (including Nigeria and Africa) for a minimal fixed sum. My royalties there were even harder to come by, for the number of books sold abroad was an unknown quantity and the price and terms under which sales actually took place were equally uncheckable.

But that mattered little to me. I had never expected to make a killing. The book was published, distributed and making its mark where it counted. In Nigeria, wherever I went I was introduced as the author of *African Revolutionary*. Journalists sought me out, and I was wined and dined extensively on each subsequent visit there, as well as elsewhere around the globe. I have been able to wear my authorship proudly, and was pleased that I had made a material, though perhaps slight, contribution to Nigeria's and the world's body of knowledge.

⁓

The struggle to make a social contribution had been at the core of my identity up until then. As I moved along from one cause to another, I would become engaged enough to satisfy myself that I was doing my bit. Yet, until the publication of *African Revolutionary*, there had never been any measurable tribute accorded me for any of my past actions or efforts. There had been a decade of floundering when I seriously questioned whether I had been doing anything worthwhile at all. Now, here was something concrete and readable for evermore. One might snort or snicker at its contents or value, review it well or badly, but there it was – for posterity.

I found further validation when Aminu made it clear that

he was obviously happy with my work. But the implied tribute that gave me the greatest pleasure came with seeing that his original ideas, expounded to me in random but carefully considered form, reappeared subsequently in his lectures, interviews and letters in a form recognizable as having been presented in *African Revolutionary*.

Although it never completely replaced the totality of the structure I had left behind in my leftist days, the effort I put into my biography of Aminu provided a form of fulfillment that gave me a strong psychological lift – a warm awareness of finally having found a tiny niche in the historical process into which I could fit.

Nigeria's Permanent Representative to the U.N., Ambassador Edwin Ogbu, arranged a launching party for my book at his official residence in Tarrytown to which he invited Nigerian friends and officials who were in New York City, as well as my friends and family. My publishers had an ample supply of books on hand for sale and autograph. The ambassador jokingly introduced me to the assembled party-goers as the head of the Feinstein family – and Mary as the essential "neck which moves the head." Aminu, in from Nigeria for the occasion, co-signed copies of the book and shared the honors. Subsequently, there were several launching parties in Nigeria, where, in my absence, Aminu starred solo and I basked in my success back in New York City.

There, in the midst of the public recognition during what seemed to be the time of my greatest glory, reality began to re-assert itself. I had to descend the mountain, but where to from High Tor? Had it been a one-shot deal, or had I moved up to a new plateau? Was it the beginning of a new career? Here I was still in mid-life. I had to think of continuity – what to do with the rest of my life?

CHAPTER TWELVE

LAUNCHING A NEW PROJECT

"I was to return to Nigeria, ready to deal with the anticipated volumes of the ambassador's notes and to pump him dry of all his memories of the events and people of the first military decade."

By 1973, the year that *African Revolutionary* was published, Fred had graduated from Swarthmore, had completed two years of teaching at an elementary school in a disadvantaged neighborhood, and was then in law school. Nancy had her bachelor's degree after switching from liberal arts in Swarthmore to fine arts at Berkeley without stopping to take a breath and had begun a doctoral program in clinical psychology.

The empty nest created something of a void in our household, but our pre-occupation with Nigeria continued to fill a good part of it. Mary was still easily intermeshing her interior design jobs with her role as homemaker, and I was continuing with my relatively full and successful dental practice. I was also wallowing in the relaxation that came with the absence of deadlines to meet, but still excited by the new avenue of release I had found to register my bits and shards of ideas as they came to me in what I saw then as spurts of creative energy.

No longer heavily immersed in organized political activity, I realized that for me, resort to the writing process had become a worthy and satisfying substitute outlet. Although it was not a complete replacement for the totality of my prior system of thought, it was far closer to answering that need than anything I had encountered up then. The exhilaration that came with reaching that plateau was sustaining me.

Mary's perpetual exuberance saw to it that our social life resumed its feverish pace, even as I tried to catch up on all the reading I had so neglected while working on the book.

In 1974 we found a delightful house to rent for the three summer months on the Mediterranean island of Ibiza off the Costa Brava of Spain, where our children and friends of both our generations spent a varying amount of time as suited their fancy. We ran it as a cooperative so that no one of us was burdened with entertaining the others. Each individual chipped in a small sum toward the rent and his or her share of the food costs, and everyone joined in with the cooking and household chores.

Along with tennis, swimming and socializing, I managed to find enough time to continue to examine the broadening hori- zons for my changing concepts of democracy and socialism, and for my life generally. I tried putting my new perspectives down on paper in the form of a rather extensive essay, tearing apart the unified theory that had dominated my thinking for so much of my youth, while trying to erect a substitute for it, using the recent Portuguese revolution and my expanded contacts with the developing countries of Africa as my research models.

Africa was still uppermost in my mind, but the Portugal of that particular time was racked with radical change that seemed to emanate from its bowels, causing that nation to regurgitate its colonies without resort to the violence that had been the benchmark of the fascist Caetano regime. I had often anticipated that some political form between capitalism and socialism would emerge. Was this the moment?

⚜

I took time to sort out my troubled and fuzzy political thoughts, exploring new fields, hoping to unearth a new theme that could once again be engrossing enough for me to continue finding excitement in the search for greater enlightenment; where I could be motivated enough to try to impart any knowledge picked up along the way to others – if anyone would listen. I had come to value the search process, not solely its end product.

The Aminu Kano book had carried me through 1973, but here it was 1974 and on into 1975. The Nigerian military was holding firm since their first coup in January 1966, despite the severe upheavals that followed. These included a second coup in July of that same year and then, within a year after that, a civil war which lasted from 1967 until 1970. The armed forces remained in the saddle.

But in July of 1975, while General Gowon, the head of state, was attending an international conference in Uganda, a group of army officers back in Nigeria decided that it was time for yet another change and staged a third coup, with the widespread existing corruption as their rationalization. Many federal commissioners and military governors and their subordinates had been living ostentatiously off the nation's recently acquired oil money, and Gowon, though apparently unimpeachable and upright himself, hadn't felt strong enough to get rid of them – previous promises to do so not withstanding.

Murtala Mohammed, the newly installed chief of state, proved to be a gung-ho, get-things-done executive who immediately established his break-the-gridlock image by imposing involuntary retirement on many of the nation's most experienced civil servants and top diplomats, many of whom I counted as friends.

Ambassador Edwin Ogbu was among them. Prior to his assignment to the U.N., Ogbu had been a permanent secretary in a succession of ministries at the highest level of the civil service. Under the military regime of the time, this position was the equivalent of minister. Yet he was one of those who were retired, apparently to create or deepen the image of Murtala as a new broom sweeping clean.

Ogbu had kept fairly extensive notes of the period, and could be a fertile primary source of information. Since his retirement would probably leave him with considerable spare time, I thought why not tap into this for a book on Nigeria's first decade of military rule? We discussed the possibilities of such a project and came up with the idea of co-writing a book on the period. I had some doubts that he would be able to organize himself sufficiently to really give it a serious effort but felt that I could step into the breach if or when needed, so long as he remained closely connected to the effort.

Together we broached the subject with a Nigerian publisher known to both of us. The publisher was quite ready to sign a contract, since no advance was suggested and his commitment would be to a finished manuscript that he could reject if he felt it unworthy. However, he added another proviso: Since I was not Nigerian, and Edwin, although well-educated with a masters' degree from Stanford University, was not an academic, why not add another co-author, a Nigerian social scientist? Sounded good to us, for neither of us was averse to lessening the load.

Ogbu returned to Nigeria, and I began the arduous task of research. When the summer solstice of 1976 rolled around, I was to return to Nigeria, ready to deal with the anticipated volumes of Edwin's notes and to pump him dry of all his memories of the events and people of the first military decade. Then, we were to search out and convince a third collaborator to join us.

⚜

In February, 1975, just as we were putting this ambitious schedule into place, General Murtala Mohammed was assassinated during a fourth, but this time failed, coup attempt. Though his regime survived, he did not. However, since his next in line, General Obasanjo, gave no indication that the senior civil servants dropped by Murtala would be reinstated, we continued according to plan.

Mary and I were to meet Ogbu in Lagos, then travel by air to Enugu, the capital of Nigeria's East-Central State at the time, and overland to Edwin's village home in Utonkon in Benue-Plateau State. But before we set out, Edwin felt that as a former major diplomat, privy to important state affairs, contemplating a book about his time in service, to be co-written by the biographer of the gadfly Aminu Kano, it would be wise to check whether the powers-that-be had any objections. He had mentioned it briefly to General Obasanjo, who had expressed some reservations, but referred him to Inspector General M. D. Yusufu, in charge of state security matters.

At Yusufu's home or office (I couldn't quite figure out which), we were led into a large reception room with sofas and chairs lining the walls, as is the customary Nigerian interior design style. The lights were dimmed, apparently not for the sake of ambiance, but creating an ominous aura of suspense nevertheless, and a feeling we were being watched. A few minutes after arrival, my night vision took over and I was able to make out the silhouettes of a half-dozen people waiting to see the inspector general.

At that point I could only think of what it would have been like to be waiting to be ushered into the inner sanctum of our American counterpart, security ogre J. Edgar Hoover. We had been there nearly an hour when someone came out to apologize for keeping all of us waiting. He said that Yusufu had been called away for an emergency and asked if Edwin and I would return at 10:00 the following morning.

I didn't know whether to feel anger or fear at the time, but was much relieved the next morning when a surprisingly disarming chief national security officer emerged right on time to joke and laugh with us and eventually dismiss our concerns. Parenthetically, he turned out to be a close friend and admirer of Aminu Kano, and subsequently he became a fast friend of ours and still is, despite his fearsome reputation.

En route from Enugu to Utonkon, we passed by the University of Nigeria, at Nsukka, which seemed a likely place to seek out our social scientist. He materialized in the form of Professor Sampson Ukpabi, a military historian with solid credentials who had been a colonel on the Biafran side in Nigeria's 1967-70 War of Secession, a period that fell well within the military decade we were examining.

This was a big plus for us, for Ambassador Ogbu had represented the federal government at the U.N. during the civil war period, and I had been among those who considered that the attempt at secession on the part of the Ibos was both undesirable and futile in the face of General Gowon's genuine attempt at reconciliation within the framework of One Nigeria.

At that time I was strongly declaiming against the one-sided public relations image of the war we were seeing in the Western World – a picture of the massacre of starving Ibo freedom fighters. Though I recognized the complex nature of the struggle and felt the tragic loss of life and horrible effects of the war, I also felt there was enough guilt to go around on both sides. The intransigence of the Ibo leadership was inexcusably prolonging the civil war's catastrophic effects. I wrote long serious letters to the *New York Times* and the *Village Voice*, attempting to correct these misapprehensions. My letters were completely ignored.

Getting Ukpabi on board provided some balance for our project, with him serving as third leg of our creative tripod. We wanted all views to be presented. He was pleased that we had sought him out and said the project appealed to him but he was working on something else at that moment. We ended up agreeing to a schedule that would have him review our work and plan his own contribution within the next six months to a year, and then activate his own contributions thereafter.

Plans for my second major literary effort were well on their way, although I hadn't a clue how to approach a book collaboration like this.

⚜

Mary and I continued our journey to Edwin's hometown where we were to combine a social visit with a serious attempt to record his experiences during the years under scrutiny. The last leg of our journey to Utonkon proved to be the equivalent of eighteen miles of cross-country travel, for it was over the worst road I had ever experienced up to then or since.

Some years later the road was leveled and rendered quite passable, but back then it was hell.

The far northern sector of Nigeria, where we had spent the bulk of our time while working on *African Revolutionary*, is peopled mostly by Muslims. By custom and religion the men there are permitted up to four wives, but only if they are able to support them and treat them all as equals – a difficult balancing act at best.

In Utonkon, in the Middle Belt of Nigeria, the predominant religion was Christianity but in practice that hardly limited the males to a monogamous existence. Back in New York we had met two of the ambassador's wives. In the village we met two others and discovered there was a total of eleven wives scattered around the globe, and close to thirty children. I must report, though, that Edwin was a staunch family man and was pledged to provide each and every one of his offspring with schooling to the limits of his or her capacity.

The room reserved for us in Utonkon had the only electric light visible in the Ogbu compound, a bulb powered by a private generator. We connected a small fan to it after retiring each night, making a stab at mitigating the oppressive heat and humidity. The remainder of our time we spent outdoors.

Victoria, Edwin's senior wife, whom we had known well back in New York while her husband was serving at the U.N. had been anxiously awaiting our arrival, concerned that we might find things a bit too primitive and uncomfortable. When, after a few days, Mary asked her pointedly if she missed the excitement of The Big Apple, she unhesitatingly responded, *"No."*

"But don't you prefer living in the relative luxury of the Western World, with all its wonderful conveniences?" Mary asked. Again the answer was "No". Asked why not, Victoria responded simply, "Mary, this my home", and went back to carrying the muddy water from the stream below the village, cooking over the open fire and bashing the clothes clean on the rocks on the banks alongside the stream.

While in Utonkon, the ambassador, though sophisticated and armed with a prestigious graduate degree, spent a good part of his day in front of his abode, literally attired in animal skins, seated under a shade of palm fronds, drinking palm wine with the townspeople. When the occasion arose, he sat in similar repose in judgment of any of his fellow villagers (most of whom were blood relatives) who had breached their accepted code of behavior, or who had come into conflict with another neighbor. On one such occasion, one party to a conflict claimed that several recent mysterious illnesses and deaths that had occurred in his family were obviously the response of the gods to his wife's infidelity, and he was demanding that some restitution be made as recognition of the guilt of his wife and her lover. This, in turn, he felt, would stop the rash of deaths. (All of this despite the Methodist Church's inroads into the village.)

In his infinite wisdom, Edwin accepted the causal relationship of the events outlined by the plaintiff and granted him relief. His judgment was to require the defendants to twirl two chickens overhead a defined number of times, after which the chickens were handed over to the plaintiff. This decision seemed to satisfy all parties concerned, for the accused were relieved of their burden of guilt while the offended party was vindicated, and at the same time the oppressive curse on his family was lifted.

After Edwin translated and explained the informal trial to Mary and me, the spellbound audience, Mary asked, "Do you really believe the events occurred as outlined?" "Of course", he responded, with a trace of a smile on his face. "What would your fellow diplomats at the U.N. think of such hijinx?" Mary pressed. He just shrugged his shoulders, his smile broadened slightly and he answered, *"Well, I don't try that kind of solution on them, do I?"*

Mary made herself quite at home, befriended a number of the women who lived in and around the Ogbu compound and danced on what very much resembled a conga line during one of their celebrations. But her efforts to introduce Western ways of thinking to the women of the community were not that successful. She pointed out to Edwin that much time and effort was wasted as the ends of the women's wrap-around skirts constantly unraveled at the waist and had to be rearranged and retucked.

"Why not cut or tear the upper edge of the skirt to make an actual tie at the waist to prevent it from constantly slipping open?" she suggested. Edwin said the women would be shocked and would probably think she was crazy, but suggested she show them anyway to see how they would respond. A few women gathered around Mary, listened, and watched her demonstration attentively, nodding their heads at first quizzically but then in apparent comprehension. The next day and the following days, when any of the women present at the demonstration passed her by, she would smile in greeting and hasten her pace, while self-consciously tucking her skirt in at the waist as had been done for generations.

⸎

While all this contact with a seemingly quasi-feudal society in the process of modernization was taking place, I was discovering that Edwin's hidden cache of notes was mostly tucked away in the remote recesses of his mind, with hardly any stored in cardboard cartons in the corners of his home, as I had hoped. Consequently, we spent hour after hour together while Edwin reminisced and I took detailed notes, interrupted only when some local administrative problem intruded itself or one or another of the men or women who were bringing in the cassava crop needed some advice, money or organizational help.

At the same time a truckload of young chickens had just arrived from Europe to serve as a base for an egg farm – and as the transition of a retired diplomat to gentleman farmer. It never did work out, as the chicks died off fairly quickly, and other plans for a pig farm never materialized.

⁂

The visit to the village was enlightening enough, but hardly a bonanza for our book project as I had hoped. Ogbu, Mary and I left together by road to Makurdi and thence to Kaduna and Kano much further north. We took advantage of Edwin's many key contacts along the way, garnering valuable interviews with army and civilian personnel who could contribute their personal observations and comments on their relationship to the civil war and other events both before and after.

In Kano once again, we visited with Aminu and the many people we had befriended on our previous trips, gathering what material I could from him and any of the others who were among the key players during the first ten years of military rule. My new project had begun to tighten its hold on me.

Among those we revisited was Zainab, the widow of Aminu's relative and closest friend, who had died suddenly. Since by tradition it was expected that she remarry after a three-month period of mourning, she ended up as the second wife of Ibrahim Dasuki, a prominent and quite conservative member of the Sokoto royal household.

It was quite a change for Zainab, whose former husband had been among the liberal and modernizing influences of the time, along with Aminu. Her new husband required that his wives be isolated in purdah. Despite this change, we became fast friends of the new husband and the family. Some years later, he was chosen as Sultan of Sokoto, the traditional and religious leader of roughly forty to fifty million Hausa-Fulani people of Northern Nigeria.

In an amusing sidelight, Ogbu asked us to find out why Zainab's new husband had denied him the right to greet his old friend Zainab. When we posed this question to Dasuki, his response was, "Why? Did he ever introduce me to any of his wives?"

CHAPTER THIRTEEN

MIRED IN POLITICS

*"I was losing confidence that what I had to contribute
would be worthwhile. My pen was drying up, and my collaborators
were not prodding me to continue."*

Upon our return to New York, our days were filled with catching up on neglected chores, getting back into the social swing and earning enough to support ourselves and still finance our extra-curricular jaunts. The first week or two after such an extended trip is usually devoted to discarding the junk mail, sorting out and paying bills, and writing responses to any letters demanding answers. And so it was on this occasion.

The few weeks spent in this fashion represented the tie between the two separate worlds that had become our bipolar focus. But there was a considerable overlap. We had Nigerian friends in New York City, at the U.N. and elsewhere who kept us abreast of events, political and personal, percolating back in their mother country and our adopted one, and we had many European and American friends living and working in Nigeria.

I hadn't quite realized how much my life had diverged from what had totally absorbed it in my youth. But friends and especially relatives made it quite clear that they felt they were being neglected, despite our continued attendance at the usual family weddings, bar mitzvahs and funerals when we were not abroad.

Otherwise our organizational ties were minimal. We strongly supported the liberal candidates of the Democratic party, as imperfect as many of them seemed, for at least they identified with the humanistic orientation that remained at the core of our social interactions. Our local involvement with the community continued, but only around the periphery, consisting primarily of financial support and talking up the right candidates and causes.

I still felt that my basic impulse to do what I could to bring about a more egalitarian, democratic, non-racist society, was on solid ground. What had changed for me was the battleground. I was no longer armed with all the answers, no longer so sure my direct and immediate actions would produce the desired result. But now fortified with a new outlet and new outlook, I was satisfied to follow my initial instincts and general direction.

This new orientation separated us from some of our old friends and acquaintances and brought us into contact with many others. But there were enough of our old associates who had come down a similar path and settled in the same or neighboring patches of land to provide a continuity with our past.

Contact with those few who were still marching to the dreary sectarian tunes of the past, still looking through the refracting lens that separated right from wrong by one's pro- or anti-Soviet or anti-imperialist stance, didn't arouse anger in me so much as an awareness of the futility of their actions.

It did make me wonder once again how I had been taken in over so long a period. It all seemed so obvious to me by this time. Sure, the revealed facts and changed times had contributed to this turn, but it was as though I was reading a totally revised textbook. The subsequent changes, which eventually occurred over a decade later in the now disintegrated Soviet Union, carried this revision to its logical, ultimate conclusion, namely, the rewriting of history itself. So why should I have been so surprised back then?

⚬⚬⚬

My new book project, though it was to have some personal twists, was to be essentially a recording of a history of the times, and thus would require a different approach from that of my biography of Aminu. Though I had interviewed a number of the political and military players during my stay in Nigeria, their testimony was to be used only to the extent that each interviewee had influenced the course of events or at least had been able to closely observe this history in the making.

The work was to be researched in detail, combining the above-mentioned personal testaments with already existing documents and print records: journals, newspapers, books, court records, decrees, laws. Since it was not meant as a straightforward, pedantic approach to the subject, the planned three-way collaboration was to be key to the process.

After my extensive interviews with Ogbu, I concluded that he could be counted on to fill in further details but not much more. With Ukpabi involved in other projects, the best I could hope for from him was perhaps a chapter or two, and that not without a long delay. With both of them in Nigeria and me sitting back in New York City, I realized that I was left to do the overwhelming bulk of the research and writing on my own.

I dove into it with vigor and enthusiasm, hoping to transcend my everyday pleasures and chores, to return to and repossess the passion of my involvement with the Aminu biography. I made some progress, starting with a detailed recording and analysis of the events that led up to the first military coup, the coup itself, the brief duration of Nigeria's first military regime, and what went wrong with it.

My position as an outsider gave me some neutral ground from which to work (although my previous association with Aminu led to my being referred to jokingly as a northerner by some of the Nigerians I interviewed). Within a reasonable period of time my reinvigorated literary energy produced a finished first chapter and most of the second. But there I stalled.

Active communication with Professor Ukpabi revealed that he was working on another project that included a year of research and post-graduate study at Oxford University. Not wanting to wait until he finished the year there, I had the bright idea that with another summer coming up, perhaps I could make arrangements to spend the month of June in Oxford, using the university's extensive Africana library and working with him on our collaboration.

He was spreading himself pretty thin at that point and said so, but thought that my proposal could work out if I didn't call upon too much of his time. He was able to book accommodations for Mary and me for about ten days at St. Anthony's College, where he was attached, and for the balance of the month at a bed and breakfast just across the street.

The university library, with much material not to be found elsewhere, and other facilities were all made available to me, and consequently used extensively. I was invited to audit any lecture sessions I felt were pertinent to our work on Africa; we frequented the college cafeteria, met Africanists from several countries including Poland, the USSR, France, Nigeria, and the U.S.A. Although non-matriculated, I was generally enjoying my reentry into an academic environment, this time in England's prime university, some thirty-five years after my undergraduate days.

Unfortunately, the primary reason for our trip to Oxford – namely to spend productive time working on our collaboration – did not progress as I had hoped. Professor Ukpabi vetted the work I had already done in rough draft and briefly discussed the portion of the book that was to be his primary responsibility.

Our master plan called for him to write the chapter on the Biafran War of Secession as he saw it from the Biafran front lines, then to be modified by myself until it was mutually acceptable, before we proceeded to the postwar chapters. But the time we spent working on Nigeria's First Military Decade was minimal, and it looked as though it would be quite some time before Ukpabi would get down to serious and active involvement in it.

But even with this reservation, we still had successfully woven a very pleasurable semi-holiday in with my research work, and continued this process according to plan on the other side of the English Channel, where Mary and I spent the following month or so at the country home of Parisian friends, a most intriguing old medieval farm-house one hour drive east of Paris. There were distractions once again, but I was reasonably conscientious and worked fairly well.

It wasn't until we returned home to Greenwich Village that

I began to have misgivings about the project. The cooperative effort I had envisioned hadn't materialized, at least not to the extent I had hoped. This new book project was dying on the vine. I was disappointed that all that work and time had not ripened into a finished product, but somehow it did not lessen my involvement with Nigeria.

Others engaged in works covering that period were at various stages of completion. I was losing confidence that what I had to contribute would be worthwhile. My pen was drying up, and my collaborators were not prodding me to continue. The unfinished manuscript, interviews, and research notes ended up resting comfortably at the back of my inactive files.

⁕

By 1978, politics leading to the establishment of a Second Republic in Nigeria had begun to take shape. Aminu, together with some other leading figures in the North, was involved in trying to organize a political party that would have extensive popular appeal – one that would not isolate him from the masses and that would promulgate his life-long goals of responsible, democratic and accountable government that would lead the nation to economic development, broadened education and en-lightenment.

But other, more conservative, traditional and self-serving leading lights of the North had very different ideas. They wanted the support of Aminu's millions of followers but weren't ready to accept his leadership or even his influence. In his first attempt at unity at the founding convention of the National Party of Nigeria (NPN), when it became clear that he and his principles were being marginalized, Aminu decamped with a group of his followers to form another political party, The People's Redemption Party (PRP).

For the period before and during the first Nigerian

Republic (1960-1965), Aminu's appeal was as an individual, heroic leader whose concern was for the *talakawa* or common man. But to set up and run a political organization, Aminu had gathered around him a group of idealistic but inexperienced and relatively uneducated lieutenants and sub-lieutenants – students, traders, union leaders and farmers who were to suffer hardships and deprivation for their political involvement.

As the months and years passed, the rewards of political opportunism enticed many of them away, but there always remained a well of good will toward Aminu as one who could not be bought. Aminu, in return, never condemned them for their lack of fortitude. As a result, even in the late 1970s, his influence in the rival parties remained strong.

Consequently, when the conflict within the NPN in this run-up to the Second Republic and election of a president arose, there was strong residual support for Aminu. But when he walked out of the convention hall many of these former supporters, who were then urging him to compromise his basic positions to remain within the party, once again chose the greener pastures by remaining within the NPN.

In the rest of the country, despite the imposition of constitutional restraints on the electorate in an attempt to prevent ethnic or regional dominance of one group over the others, each of the three major ethnic groups organized a party around their own local ethnic leader and then tried to reach out across state boundaries for allies. One of these parties split into two, which made a total of five parties contesting at the polls (including Aminu's PRP).

These developments in Nigeria were completely absorbing me, so that dropping the book project wasn't as upsetting as it might have been. When election time arrived in the summer of 1979 it found Mary and me on the scene, travelling all areas of Nigeria observing, asking questions, and where it wasn't too obvious, putting in a good word for Aminu.

It became clear to me that although Aminu was respected, even revered, throughout the country, including by voters in the South, there was a strong feeling that because of his uncompromising, principled stance on the side of the masses, he didn't have a chance of getting elected. People, it seemed likely, would vote for the candidate who came from their own ethnic group and who, if elected, might help their own specific regional needs.

Unfortunately, this fear of losing the election to another region prevailed throughout much of the nation among the informed as well as the uninformed. The only area where support for Aminu was overwhelming was in his home state Kano, spilling over to some extent into several contiguous states.

An odd contradiction developed during the election when Aminu's rivals tried to have him disqualified, ostensibly because he hadn't paid his income taxes! There weren't very many Nigerians who didn't have a sense that Aminu was leading an ascetic life, that he was the one politician of note who was above reproach. Yet the traditional wielders of power wanted him off the scene in an attempt to amass votes for their own parties, and this was their method of choice.

Court cases challenging these moves were protracted and finally decided in Aminu's favor. The judge held basically that Aminu had no income to tax. But the decision came only days before the election, thus bolstering the view held by many that – the semblance of democracy not-withstanding – Aminu would never be permitted to penetrate the power structure. Therefore many voters gave their allegiance to their traditional patron-client relationships rather than daring to hope for a change.

The balloting itself was rife with electoral irregularities, but each area in the country was controlled by local police and influenced accordingly. The net result was an impasse. The NPN won a clear plurality, but gained 25 percent of the vote in only twelve states.

According to the newly written constitution, without 25 percent of the votes in two-thirds of the nineteen states, the choice of president would have to be thrown to an electoral college composed of the senate, house of representatives, and local state legislatures. The contest itself thus was reduced to a count of how many delegates each candidate could buy – a considerably less democratic solution than even the skewed election could produce.

The courts were left with the decision. They finally accepted the contorted formula presented by the lawyers of the NPN, namely that since two-thirds of nineteen states is twelve and two-thirds, and since the NPN won the required 25 percent in twelve, then all they needed was 25 percent of two-thirds of another state, or one-sixth of the vote in that state. Which they had.

This obvious ruse was reluctantly accepted by the bulk of the populace as a better solution than throwing the choice of president to the electoral college, with its anticipated chaos. Awolowo, the runner-up, and his stalwarts complained bitterly and tried to appeal this solution, but to no avail.

Aminu's party, the PRP, had won about 11 percent of the national vote, and two state governorships (in Kano and neighboring Kaduna), and he evidently felt that for his party to raise any strong objections to the declared results at that point would have been destabilizing, and would not have served any useful purpose. The NPN candidate, Shehu Shagari, was installed as president, as the army returned to the barracks. Nigeria simmered down to sullen national acceptance.

CHAPTER FOURTEEN

SLOWING DOWN

*"The difficulty with this new stage in my life was
not too much spare time, but not enough."*

Home once again, I found myself in the midst of a personally
intriguing but perhaps less-than-cataclysmic change. To all
the soul searching, disorientation and angst I had gone
through during my life-time and which assumedly would
continue uninterruptedly into the indefinite future, was
added a new dimension: Retirement.

Vague thoughts about possible retirement suddenly
became quite immediate in the spring of 1980, when we called
upon the real estate agent who rented our city apartment for
us each summer in order to provide the wherewithal for our
jaunts around the globe. This time he casually asked whether
we would be interested in selling rather renting our town

house. Before we could reject this suggestion out of hand, he mentioned a proposed selling price. Mary and I looked at each other and smiled. At that price we couldn't afford to live there anymore.

Mary was never one to wait for events to fall into place. She had to push them there. That very day she peeked through the slightly opened door of a cooperative loft apartment in the Village that she had found in the real estate listings. Within three weeks we had a contract for the purchase of the apartment. Within three months our house was sold. Within four months we moved.

The purchase price for the loft was one-third the selling price for the house. The remaining two-thirds could serve as the financial basis for my retirement. Add to that the income from our small savings and the sale price for my dental practice, and we could just about swing a retirement without cutting into our standard of living. Surely a living testimony to the validity of Mary's philosophy; to wit, if you think positively and live long enough, all good things will come to pass. Particularly if you don't wait, but rush out to meet them. So why not retirement?

⚜

The widespread fear of entering this new stage I mused, was based on the concept that work, a major focus of one's life, was to be suddenly terminated. It was often assumed that when faced with the resultant plethora of additional time on one's hands, the effect would be demoralizing. With Africa and the prospect of finding more time for writing before me, however, this possibility didn't faze me one bit.

I did wonder, however, how such a change in my relationship to work would affect me personally. I had never feared the idea of retirement. Though I had always enjoyed my profession and the relationships that grew out of it, and felt that my work was unquestionably socially useful, I had never made it the all-pervasive focus that so many professionals do.

But I saw myself in many roles: in relation to those around me (family, friends and acquaintances); as a dental professional; as a political animal; and then, as an Africanist. In each of these areas, I felt that my contributions to the welfare of others and to society had been productive, while I myself was deriving some needed social and self-esteem in exchange. So why should there be any difficulty in dropping one of these identities and allowing my other pursuits to take up the slack?

I knew that with retirement would come an imperceptible shift in emphasis from participation to observation. Though an appreciation of the sensual was never the paramount goal in my life, I could still enjoy an increase in interpersonal contacts and find diversion in the arts an escape. When not so occupied, I reasoned, I could return to my basic reality, the realm of ideas, whether work-related or avocational.

But I didn't find the shift that easy. A life-time of habits and built-in values carried over. Relax and enjoy sounded good, but with my life dominated by meaning and achievement how could I derive the depth of self-satisfaction I was looking for, from either the passive accumulation of further knowledge or from mere satisfaction of the senses?

My need for some form of creative engagement thus became even greater. Could my avocation replace my vocation? The void that opened up when I no longer had that solid block of time I had been expending at the dental chair had to be filled. To my dismay, I found that little chores and administrative details seemed to rush to fill the vacuum at a more rapid pace than any attempts at increased literary output.

My wonderful career-long nurse-assistant-friend in the office was no longer there to write my checks, answer correspondence and generally make life easier for me. And if I was no longer putting in a hard day's work in the office, Mary certainly could expect a greater degree of sharing of our household affairs. She continued to handle the lioness' share of our chores, but now there was more together time, and chauffeuring, to the point where the free hours gained from no longer maintaining an office seemed to vanish. My slowly diminishing physical capacities stole into that void as well.

I wrote in my sometime journal:

> The retirement process seems to place the inanities and chores needed just to tread water, to remain in place, in much sharper focus. Not only do we have to perform these chores but so much of our lives is spent in talking about them – what we eat for breakfast, where we ate it, at what pace we walk, *ad infinitum*. When we were younger we just did these things. We didn't think of them as subjects for prolonged conversations. We were engaged in preparing for life, then in living it. Now, in retirement, we talk about the minutiae of it.

> I can sit in a social group at a dinner party, listen to the chatter, and somehow I hear little beyond that. I don't know how I can contribute, so I listen, but barely. Yet I feel warmly toward the people involved and don't lose respect.

> But at this stage in life I wonder, is this the basic way people are expected to relate to one another as individuals or as a group? Discussing politics, society? Is this a lost art or just a bore? Am I being misanthropic? On a one-on-one basis, communication is much more intimate

and meaningful. Is my preoccupation with writing just another form of this more pleasant dialogue, or is it a more restricting form of separation and isolation?

My years will be more and more limited now, and my search for a purpose is yielding little of solace. Why can't I learn to better enjoy these inanities of living? To relax in the knowledge that there is no other perceivable meaning to our existence – that it is merely a process with a beginning, an end, and occasionally a middle – and try to get some pleasure out of my contacts with people as long as I am around and enjoy delving into the thoughts of those around me, or even my own?

The difficulty with this new stage in my life was not too much spare time, but not enough. My feeling of connectedness was being threatened, and I was troubled by this change in my way of relating.

Here I had so looked forward to all the additional time I would have to write. Yet when it was upon me I was floundering and allowing so many other intrusions upon my time, that rather than excitedly surging ahead with the anticipated flurry of literary production, I found my days flitting by without my even settling on a new project. I accepted this and even welcomed it for a short time, convinced that I needed the break to readjust, but it didn't take long for my restlessness to take over once again.

Obviously I was conflicted not only by the increase in my leisure time, but also by this stage in my life. As the years of my retirement surrounded me, I just slipped from day to day and staggered into the next month, the next year, carrying this burden without any definitive resolution.

The contemplated release from the responsibility of caring for the dental health of the world around me somehow eluded me. During my first year of official retirement I spent one to two days per week in the office to effect a smooth transfer of my practice to my successor. I had sold it for a modest sum to a young woman who had been working for me part time for several years. Her work during that period had been quite satisfactory and most of the patients had gotten to know her.

This plan of action meshed neatly with my primary goal of ensuring that my patients could continue getting high-quality care if they chose to remain with the practice. By and large, they had confidence in my work and assumed they could depend on my judgment and recommendation. The one-year transition period was meant to keep as many of them as possible in the practice.

That process, together with the homework necessary to close out my accounts, sopped up most of my spare time for that year anyway. However, it was accompanied by an unexpected ambivalence on my part. I was anxious for the transition to be smooth, but its successful execution shook the feeling of indispensability imparted to me by my patients over the years. It just seemed too easy to transfer this indispensability to another. A bit of a shock after a life-time of assurance to the contrary.

Desk time in my study gradually took over from dental-chair time as my day-time preoccupation, but the creative literary output I looked forward to over the years was largely crowded out by those new responsibilities: bills to pay, forms to fill out and even long-neglected letter writing. And contrary to the myth of the wife marrying her husband "for better or worse but not for lunch," Mary welcomed our additional time together.

A well of tolerance and respect as well as room for differences had evidently been built up over the years, so that in my new incarnation, the two of us could share more of the chores, driving one another about town on errands without concern about parking. We could still travel abroad relatively freely for although Mary continued working she could easily adjust her free-lance work time to conform to our joint vacation needs and desires.

Still, I found myself increasingly mired in morbid introspection – questioning the value of my efforts and, indeed, the premises of my life-long search for meaning and purpose. This state of mind had built up gradually, dating as far back as the late 1970s when the glow of being a published writer began to fade. It would come in waves. Involvement in my personal life, pride in family, camaraderie with friends would perk me up. Listening to music, either at concerts, operas, or even on radio and television could always be counted on to bolster my sagging spirits.

But events on the national and international fronts had the opposite effect. Nigerian government leaders were wallowing in corruption. No real observable, principled political organization was taking hold. There was no apparent sign of any resolution to the myriad problems in the offing. Africa and most developing countries appeared to be stagnating. These disappointments – this sense of dreams unrealized and promise unfulfilled – left me depressed, comforted only when I shifted my thoughts back to my personal good fortune.

CHAPTER FIFTEEN

UNDER THE SAIL AGAIN

*"We hoped to help break down the barriers to a more informed
understanding between the residents of both nations through a
Nigerian-American joint conference to introduce Americans
and Nigerians to each other's ways of thinking."*

During those years, while flailing about in my hunt for a way
to stay in touch with the world as I knew it, it struck me that
back home in New York the people around me – otherwise
fairly well informed – knew very little, practically nothing,
about the Africa that had so engrossed me for some fifteen or
sixteen years.

The Africa on which I had concentrated so much was out
there, and I and my friends and acquaintances were here. I
felt that some justification for my extended interest was in
order. Positioned as I was explain the one world to the other,

I tried putting together an informal slide show to present to several informal groups, thereby exposing my new world to my old. I enjoyed some success in bringing this presentation to school children, who showed a more lively interest than adult groups I spoke to. But I found that lecturing at this level hardly satisfied my desire for involvement. I was thinking more along organizational lines.

⚜

Just about that time, by coincidence, I received a letter from a young Nigerian teaching at the college level in New Jersey, asking whether I would be interested in helping to organize an academic conference to analyze and discuss Nigerian-American relations. Although I was seeking a forum broader than academia – something more along intercultural lines – I called him.

We met and incorporated our suggestions into a broader idea for an organization devoted to Nigerian-American friendships. I contacted many friends to discuss this idea, as well as patients, black and white, Nigerians and Americans, resident in the New York City area, and even the Nigerian-American Chamber of Commerce.

This last group responded cautiously, apparently concerned that our jurisdictions might overlap, but they cooperated when I made it abundantly clear that the organization we had in mind was to be primarily cultural, concerned with business in only a peripheral way. Thus was born the Nigerian American Friendship Society.

The first organizational meeting was held in our home, but the group rapidly grew beyond these confines. Percy Sutton, a prominent leader of the African-American community was elected chairman of the board; I served as president. Our plans included development of a Nigeria House as a local showcase for Nigerian culture, publication of a journal, possible sponsorship of tours to Nigeria and the rest of Africa, and finally, a Nigerian American joint conference to introduce Americans and Nigerians to each other's ways of thinking.

In this way we hoped to help break down the barriers to a more informed understanding between the residents of both nations; to bring black and white together in the U.S. and to help bring Nigerians of different ethnic backgrounds and regions together in Nigeria, helping to heal any wounds that might be lingering from their recent civil war, and giving all a stronger sense of themselves as part of their respective nations.

◦◦◦

It was this concept of a conference that took hold as our first major effort. If the conference was successful it would be an enlightening reward in itself, as well as a platform for a national organization with chapters in urban centers throughout the nation and a counterpart organization in Nigeria.

Our theme, "Nigeria-America: Toward an Era of Cooperation and Progress", would permit us to examine and compare areas such as arts, constitution, technology transfer, and so forth in the two countries, with leaders in each field from both nations presenting papers. Our plans for the conference, to be held in January, 1980, were grandiose and required intensive preparation and cooperation.

For a conference on this scale to be successful we would have to be able to attract leading lights from both countries as well as ample financing. In order to remain independent, we had to exclude monetary assistance from both governments, thus restricting our possibilities for funding to individuals or corporations. In this, Mary did a heroic job, coordinating the organizational work and securing the important financing from a number of corporations.

We were phenomenally successful with our preparations. Both countries cooperated wholeheartedly, starting with President Jimmy Carter, who agreed to attend. The governor of the Bank of Nigeria, Ola Vincent, and the director of the U.S. Import Export Bank, T. DeSaint Phalle, were to discuss our financial relations. Two prominent economists, Professor Sayre Schatz of Temple University, who had done extensive studies on Nigerian capitalism, and Professor Anne Seidman of Clark University, were to add their comments.

Other authorities in their respective fields were recruited: Discussing technology transfer were Dr. Jibril Aminu on the governmental level and Dr. Aaron Segal then with the National Science Foundation. at the time as commentators. Professor Chinua Achebe, the leading Nigerian novelist, represented the arts and literature. Diplomats scheduled as speakers included Donald Easum, former U.S. ambassador to Nigeria and president of the African-American Institute at the time, and ambassadors Andrew Young from the U.S. and Edwin Ogbu from Nigeria, both former permanent representatives to the U.N.

⁂

The conference was well attended and came off fabulously. But serious organizational and political problems had emerged behind the scene. Some African-Americans active in the organization believed that their association with the Nigerian American Friendship Society would open a path for personal business opportunities in oil-rich Nigeria and cared little for the inter-cultural aspects that were supposed to be our core activity.

These few chose to try to diminish the leadership role of Mary and myself and our supporters in order to gain what they perceived to be the prestige of office and to change the basic purpose of the organization by painting the Nigerian American Friendship Society as a black solidarity group. There was an obvious attempt within this faction to marginalize our role (Mary's more so than mine) at the conference itself.

Even before the eminently successful conclusion of the conference, Mary and I had decided it would be too much for us to continue under the circumstances. It was quite unpleasant and certainly not a battlefield on which we would choose to fight. We did actively continue with our leading role in the conference itself, but at its conclusion, we quietly withdrew from leadership by not standing for re-election.

After our withdrawal, the society continued just so long as the treasury surplus we had left them lasted, after which the organization gradually disappeared from view.

Although the conference left a good impression with those who were involved, it was a most unpleasant ending for the sponsoring organization. The downward course of Nigeria's political and economic development since then didn't help much either , but at the time Nigerian American friendship was a worthy enough goal – or so we had thought.

Nancy, Aminu Kano and Mary, 1963

Former Sultan Dasuki of Sokoto and Mary, 1984

Mallam Aminu Kano at his office, 1971

CHAPTER SIXTEEN

SET ADRIFT

*"In mid-April, 1983, the phone rang in the wee hours of
the morning. I could not have been more stunned when I finally
made out what the caller was saying: Aminu is dead!"*

While we were engaged in organizing the conference here at
home, conditions in Nigeria continued to deteriorate. Shehu
Shagari's term of office as president, begun in 1979, was
characterized by corruption and dalliance with the people's
funds, extending from federal through state and local levels,
from high to low. Everyone seemed to be dipping his hand
into the public till to enrich himself or the party coffers, with
no one prepared to shout "Stop".

I was sorely disappointed with this state of affairs, but felt
that if ever there was to be any significant change, Aminu and
his party would hold the key.

Our biennial trips to Nigeria were still a primary focus for us, but under the circumstances Aminu's trips to New York became less and less frequent. Our written correspondence, never very consistent, became even less so. I realized that he was immersed in time- and attention-consuming day-to-day party organization, as well as the affairs of the two states under the control of the Peoples' Redemption Party (PRP). But I soon found that my distant mentor was involved in more than simple administrative tasks. The problems that he had with the Northern Elements Progressive Union (NEPU), his party during Nigeria's First Republic, had returned to plague him in the Second.

The political elite were continuing and intensifying their concentration on improving their own individual lot, with no noticeable concern for national economic development, the improvement of the living standards of the masses or accountability to those who had put them in their leadership positions. And sad to say, Aminu's lieutenants were not immune to the enticements of this mode of governing.

The two elected PRP governors came into conflict with Aminu and the party leadership almost immediately after taking office. Governor Balarabe Musa in Kaduna, coming in from the left field of political thought, ignored the admonitions of Aminu and the party leaders to compromise with the NPN (National Party of Nigeria) which controlled the state legislature in order to be able to govern with a semblance of order. After an extended stand-off, with Musa unable to gain legislative acceptance for his cabinet and administrative appointees, the legislature resolved the impasse by voting to impeach and remove the newly elected governor from office.

In Kano the PRP completely dominated both the state legislative and executive branches. However, Governor Abubakar Rimi, reinforced by what he saw as an independent power base, used key appointments as patronage plums to bolster his position. Contrary to Aminu's advice and directives to remain unaligned he began meeting with other opposition state governors to form a loose alliance against the ruling party. Aminu felt that these moves were opportunistic and threatened to weaken the party's independent status.

As in NEPU years, Aminu was unable to build an effective unified political organization, despite his direct personal emotional appeal to the millions of his followers. When many of his cadres abandoned Aminu's principled positions, a dissident faction developed, led by Kano Governor Rimi. The split widened to the point of no return.

By the time the four-year terms (1979-83) of the legislators and the president of Nigeria's Second Republic were almost over and the nation was once again facing a national election, Aminu's PRP was in shreds, and Aminu, himself, was seriously ill.

❦

Aminu had lost consciousness on several occasions and had been to England for extended diagnostic and treatment visits. According to the testimony of the loyalists who had remained faithful, it seemed he was losing his grip. His attention to detail was inconsistent and he was leaning more and more heavily on the leadership and advice of his remaining loyal lieutenants, even though some of these were paying closer attention to their own personal fortunes than to the principles and political fate of their party.

In Aminu's home state, Kano, Governor Abubakar Rimi was busy trying to win over dissident PRP voters to a new rival party he had formed after he was rejected by the PRP. Through dubious and intimidating tactics, Sabo Bakin-Zuwo and his cohorts were occupied behind the scenes with capturing control of what was left of the state party apparatus, ultimately capturing its nomination and his election as governor of Kano State, defeating the incumbent Rimi.

Though still professing undying loyalty to Aminu and his principles, Bakin-Zuwo's actions belied his words. Aminu was the party's presidential candidate once again, but instead of presenting the unified face of a principled party of the masses triumphantly marching forward toward greater and greater influence, Aminu and the party core found themselves struggling to retain a modicum of loyalty to Aminu and his ideals.

During the early months of 1983, while in the midst of all his physical ailments and political problems, Aminu chose to come to New York City under the watchful eye of Musa Musawa, for a brief period of recuperation. Musa was a man whose past in the External Affairs Ministry was somewhat suspect but who nevertheless had remained loyal to Aminu, and was his party's gubernatorial candidate for Kaduna State.

Aminu and I spent a good part of the visit together and chatted at length. As optimistic as ever, he reassured me that he was in good health. His party was rebuilding for the future, he said, and despite the opportunistic tendencies of so much of the leadership in the party, the masses still supported him fervently.

But there was a strange separation from us and our friend, as though he spoke from another room or through a veil. He clung to Mary and me, not wanting to part from our company each time we saw him. Nor was he anxious to return to the fray back home, as he always had been in the past. Only in retrospect did it occur to me that his visit and his behavior while here in New York City was probably his way of saying good-bye.

Christie and Chinua Achebe

Ambassador Donald Easum, 1983

In mid-April, 1983, the phone rang in the wee hours of the morning. It was Fatima Wali, our young Nigerian friend and daughter of Aminu's closest friend back in the 1960s, calling from Minnesota where she was studying architecture. She was weeping and could hardly form her words. I could not have been more stunned when I finally made out what she was moaning.

"Aminu is dead! Aminu is dead!"

"Are you sure? We were told this very same news last week and it turned to be just a rumor."

"I know, I know, but I just got a phone call from Kano, and this time it's true! What will we do now? We need him so", she wailed.

We called Kano. It was true. A friend said that Shatu, his wife, had seen him the night before, just as he was retiring. He never woke up. Apparently one of his recurrent malaria attacks had finally reached his brain and proven fatal. Aminu, the only leader on the scene who could possibly bring some hope to Nigeria, had died.

Several people around him attested to strange behavior on his part over the last week or two of his life. One friend was called by Aminu on the very night he passed away to reconcile a dispute that had bedeviled them for many years. Aminu concluded with the admonition, *"We don't live forever, you know."* Another said that three days prior to his death he had raised three fingers when asked how he felt.

Mary and I joined the hand-wringing. I couldn't believe he was really gone, nor conceive of a world without him. I had not fully realized until then how much of my life I had built around him. There was, first of all, the sense of the deep personal loss of a dear, dear friend. On his past visits I had assumed personal responsibility for taking him to visit the most highly respected doctors in New York (though in the last years of his life he was under the care of competent British physicians).

As so often in such cases, there were strong guilt feelings. I wondered if there was anything I could possibly have done to save him. But death is so irrevocable. I just had to reconcile myself to its stark reality. For a full day and night I could think of nothing else and tried not to sink into a disorienting depression. Should I pick up and run off to Kano? Muslims, like Jews, bury their dead within twenty-four hours.

The Nigerian government and populace reacted quickly by suspending business to mourn the loss of the man who had embodied the national conscience for so many years. The President, the Vice-president, all the dignitaries of the nation, its traditional leaders and hundreds of thousands of people massed to pay homage.

Finally, I settled for sending a condolence note:

Dear Shatu and Family:

...You well know how close Mallam Aminu has been to us over more than two decades. He has been colleague, friend, brother and source of great inspiration. He changed the entire course of our lives, made us aware of the depth and dimensions of the struggle for justice for the underprivileged and down-trodden in Africa and throughout the world. He introduced us to a world which was at first strange and exciting, then involving to the point of becoming the major focus of our lives.

In 1963 and thereafter, on alternate years, we traveled to Africa, always making Nigeria the hub of our trip. The country became our adopted land, and Aminu, you, and the children our family. Our Nigerian friends grew in number, as those who now know us throughout Nigeria's nineteen states and the U.S.A. will attest.

The essence of Aminu's life will live on - which should give you, Asmau and the children some consolation, but we all will miss the man. I feel as though a huge piece of me was just torn out of my flesh, leaving a deep hole that can never be filled. My life will never again be the same.

Let us hope that the future will recognize your husband's true worth and that Nigeria will carry on in his spirit. It is this possibility that sustains us in this period. You and the family should be able to take some solace in these thoughts as well . . .

Moving tributes were forthcoming, from the president of the nation on down. I sent a memorial essay to West Africa magazine which was printed in full. I wanted to share my grief with the world, and my determination that Aminu would continue to live even after death. But there was no one in New York, Nigerian or otherwise, who had a sense of what had passed between Aminu and myself – except perhaps Mary, and she was mourning almost as deeply as I was. But for Mary, I felt completely isolated.

CHAPTER SEVENTEEN

COMPLETING THE WORK

*"After some weeks in shock, my way of dealing with Aminu's death was to bury myself in the task of writing the revised and updated version of **African Revolutionary**, in the hope that it could help keep Aminu's vision alive."*

Obviously, we would have to miss Aminu's funeral, but we pushed up our next visit to Nigeria to May, though it had been planned originally for the summer national elections. Until then, I couldn't shake my feeling of loss. Not only had Aminu, the person, penetrated my deepest consciousness, but knowing him and what he was had enabled me to find a new focus. He had given me a whole new sense of relating to the world after years of uneasy disorientation, living from day to day looking for some satisfying way to tie together my pragmatic actions into a unifying credo.

I had finally found it and desperately wanted to hold on. With Aminu gone, I had to try to dissociate the man from his principles and ideas. It wasn't easy. I just had to keep Aminu alive to retain the continuity of the path I had wandered onto over a lifetime; to give some semblance of meaning to my life with one day leading logically into the next, one event leading to another.

In Kano once again, we paid our condolences to Aminu's family and all of his friends and political confrere. We sadly discussed the vacuum that Aminu had left. Everyone agreed that my associations with Aminu Kano and Nigeria should logically include a written treatment of the last decade of this remarkable life, from 1973 (the year *African Revolutionary* was published) to his death in April, 1983.

⁂

I believed that a second volume, or perhaps or an updated edition of the first book, could provide a fitting tribute to Aminu's turbulent life, could help perpetuate the ideals of Aminu-ism and could enable me to continue my humble contribution to society, while coincidentally permitting me to regain my precarious foothold on my own life. Where to from there would be a question I could resolve while I was writing.

By this time I had learned the hard way to throw my support to leaders who were promulgating the causes I believed in, and to withdraw that support when or if they deserted that path for opportunistic or other reasons. I knew how to seek out other worthy allies who were still intent upon achieving our original goals. But in this very special case, where the leader left the scene without having strayed, I was hard put to find a replacement.

Even Aminu had not been able to establish a line of succession among progressive Nigerians. There were others who like myself were groping for a replacement, but there was no one on the scene who could step into his shoes. Chinua Achebe, Nigeria's leading novelist and poet put it this way:

> The importance... of people like Aminu Kano (or Mahatma Gandhi) is not that every politician can become like them, for that would be... totally unrealistic. But the monumental fact is that [they]... were real, not angels in heaven. Nigeria cannot be the same again because Aminu Kano lived here.

I thought that surely from among the millions of his ardent followers some would arise to carry the torch, but Achebe apparently is right. Not every, or for that matter, any politician can be like Aminu. The nation was just not ready to accept the disembodied ideals of the man without him before them as their living symbol. The image, memories and legend would remain long after he was gone, but the future of the principles and moral code that were the underpinnings for his push toward democracy, development and equality was dubious. Only time would tell. But time waits for no one, neither me nor his beloved country.

After some weeks in shock, my way of dealing with Aminu's death was to bury myself in the task of writing the revised and updated version of *African Revolutionary* in the hope that it could help keep Aminu's vision alive.

Within nine months of Aminu's death and only four months after the much contested election of August 1983, the military again seized the reins of government. Politicians as a class were once again persona non grata. Some of them fled, some were arrested, but strings continued to be pulled from remote corners of the nation. I interviewed many of those who had remained loyal to Aminu to the end as well as many who had not.

In Kano State, I interviewed leaders from each of the political factions in the PRP. I found that I had little enthusiasm for the task. Each person I interviewed wanted to be seen as waiting in the wings for the return of civilian politics, so that the banner of Aminu could again be waved. And yet when each told the story of the preceding decade he spoke from his own self-serving point of view. Each swore post-mortem fealty to Aminu, the man and his ideas. Wherever I looked, I found shadows of the same devious maneuvering that had gone on while Aminu was still alive.

The much respected Chinua Achebe was one of the very few leading southerners of note in Nigeria who had perceived and internalized Aminu's true worth, and consequently had aligned himself with the People's Redemption Party, ending up as a vice president. Through it all, he had managed to avoid its internecine struggles.

Those few who, like Achebe, tried to continue along the path that Aminu had blazed, were discouraged and depressed and saw no real possibility for the development of a mass movement to carry on Aminu's work under the existing circumstances – at least not in the foreseeable future.

Simmering below the surface, I could clearly sense the nation's uneasiness with the realization that it was still unprepared to band together for the common good – the idea at the core of Aminu's philosophy. The nation revered the aura and the concept, but was not yet ready to immerse itself in the political process needed to flesh these out. The miserable state of affairs in Nigeria fit perfectly with my own depressed view of world events, and made it very difficult for me to concentrate on my writing. But I persevered, slowly putting the facts and my interpretations of them down on paper.

⚜

Once again I was absorbed in arduous yet engrossing research and writing. Apart from the additional ten years I had to chronicle, I also had to revisit and re-evaluate the conclusions I had made in the first edition. The summer of 1985 found me in Nigeria once again gathering interviews and examining all the printed materials I could lay my hands on.

Writing that winter was a pleasant task. With my retirement came the practice of going south with the birds and the sun for the month of February, something I had never ventured while practicing dentistry full time. I could write pretty much wherever I pleased. I had completed my notes, tapes and reference material in Nigeria, so I was able to take these with me to write while basking in the warmth of Puerto Rico or other Caribbean isles. That particular year we discovered Martinique, an especially relaxing haven, where, despite the distractions of paradise, my literary output went relatively well.

Hunting down a publisher for this, my next major literary effort, proved to be easier than anticipated. That fall during an African Studies Association Conference, I was having lunch with Professor John Paden, who by this time had become a dear friend, when we were joined by Lynn Reinner, a Colorado-based publisher of a number of titles on Africa.

When I mentioned what I was up to, she said that she would be glad to publish the revised edition if John would write a brief preface for it. Just that easy. The terms she offered were not that favorable, but it was such a relief not to have to beat around publishers' offices that I readily agreed to them.

By 1987, the American edition was ready. The publisher had modest goals for it, pricing it much higher than I wanted or thought wise. She was apparently gearing it primarily toward libraries and African Studies courses. Net result – poor sales. My experience with the first volume had toned down my expectations, but I had reserved the rights to the Nigeria market for myself and could consider a paperback edition for Nigerian distribution, knowing full well that the book would have wide market appeal there.

I approached several people who had known and respected Aminu and his work, to ask if any of them would be interested in financing and publishing such a venture. One of those approached, Aliyu Dasuki, responded in a letter from Lagos indicating interest and asking what would be involved so far as he was concerned. I wrote to him, giving all details and cost estimates as best I could.

I waited a good long time for a response, but none seemed to be forthcoming. But one day the phone rang. It was Aliyu, this time in New York City for one day. He accepted our invitation to dinner that evening. Over coffee and dessert I outlined my suggestions for the book in some detail, to include a printing in the U.S. and shipment to Nigeria. He casually put his hand in his pocket and pulled something out, saying *"Will this cover it?"* I was startled. It was a check for $25,000!

"But of course! I'll keep accurate records and send you the unused balance, with a detailed report on expenditures." When I asked what were his plans for distributions in Nigeria, he smiled and said, *"That's your problem. You work it out. I'm finished with the project and don't expect any reports or return on investment. This is my contribution to your work in keeping Aminu's spirit alive."* I knew little about this young man, save that he was apparently well heeled and that Aminu had referred to him in his diary as a devoted and loyal friend. So there I was, in the publishing business.

Everything seemed to continue to fall neatly into my lap.

But then I was left with the task of ferreting out a printer here and a distributor there in Nigeria. When I approached what I considered to be Nigeria's leading publisher, he quickly snapped up my very favorable offer. I would cover the printing costs with Aliyu's financing, and put their imprint on the paperback.

Within a few months, despite some mishaps with the printing and the shipping due to my inexperience, I managed to get the first printing delivered to them before April 1988. Book launchings in Kano, Lagos and probably Kaduna had been planned by the publishers and a group of Aminu's former disciples to coincide with the fifth anniversary of his death.

⚜

Launching a book in Nigeria usually follows a fairly set pattern, with some political overtones. Friends and well-wishers make speeches and donate sums of money, sometimes fairly large, by purchasing many copies of the book for distribution among their friends and associates, particularly if the book is political in nature, as mine was.

Flying across the Atlantic once again to participate in these parties, my thoughts were already taking shape. I was sure there would be some hitch, some letdown. In Nigeria things have a way of happening in a loose, unpredictable time frames. So different from the ways of New Yorkers where the calendar is dominated by the clock, and the hour hand by the minute hand – where the schedule is supreme.

My anticipation of foul-ups wasn't far wrong. In Kano, where the first and largest of the launchings was to take place, we headed for Abdullahi Bayero University campus where I could meet the vice-chancellor, a senior advisor to Aminu before his death, and a number of faculty members and students who had similarly been followers of Aminu.

The vice-chancellor, who was to have organized the launching on the campus, welcomed me but hemmed and hawed when it came to listing what arrangements had actually been made. It seems he was preoccupied with an impending student strike, and as a result did not think he could arrange it on campus. A few of the lesser potentates at the university talked vaguely about finding another venue for the launching, and referred me to a bookstore in the city where I could find the publisher's representative. He was just as unhelpful, indicating that he had been counting on Aminu's local supporters to put the event together.

The days flew by. One professor organized a memorial meeting with me as the principal speaker, but when I arrived I found that the police had canceled the meeting. No permit. Another member of the Federal House of Representatives from Kano promised to get something together a few weeks hence, well after Mary and I planned to leave Nigeria, but despite his eagerness he didn't have the bulk of Aminu's supporters behind him. Yet another small group of more influential friends promised a launching in Lagos a month or two later, at which time they would send us air tickets.

While marking time, my presence in Kano did make a slight splash. The Kano newspaper sent an orthodox Muslim woman reporter (whose religion forbade her to shake hands with any man) to interview me in great detail, and news reports of my arrival appeared in other magazines and newspapers. But no concrete book launching plan arose from any of it. Compounding the general ineptness was the still unstable political situation. Almost everyone hesitated to do anything, not knowing what effect a major launching of this kind would have on the general populace and not wanting to stir up the military.

Though the launching could have been non-partisan, even apolitical under those circumstances, the apprehensions prevailed and Mary and I left Nigeria disappointed, with only a vague promise of a launching at some time in the near future.

⁂

Somehow this trip felt like my last trip to Africa. Lagos and Kano felt more like a revival of frustration than a pleasant memory of past relationships renewed. Our frustrations with transportation, communication, sanitation seemed to overshadow the stimulation we had always felt in the past. Aminu was gone, with politics not far behind.

The Nigerian economy was on the rocks. What would bring us back there? A new project? A new surge in Nigeria leading up to the 1992 elections? (As of 1995 these scheduled elections still had not taken place.) Where are the signs of true stirring? Perhaps from the young blood following in Aminu's path, but where are they? A young Tanimu here, an Ahmadu Jalingo there, yet many, many more are still in the rut of personal opportunism and sycophancy, or consumed by passionate beliefs that their rewards lie in the hereafter.

I was never notified, but heard through the grapevine that the publishers finally launched the book a month or two after we returned to New York. The would-be politicians, as expected, had delivered self-serving speeches, covering themselves with Aminu's general ideas on democracy with no real suggestions as to how they proposed to achieve them.

The same chaotic, amoral lack of political direction that prevailed at the time has continued to the present, as Nigeria remains in perpetual transition from military to civilian rule, without even coming close to the path toward democracy that Aminu Kano had so clearly outlined for his nation.

CHAPTER EIGHTEEN

APPROACHING FINAL PORT

*"This nebulous tie to society and need to find social meaning
in my life still dominates my mind."*

With the completion of the second volume of *African Revolutionary*, I could once again consider myself retired. My lack of
enthusiasm for the things that had gripped me in the past
was coupled with a stronger and stronger urge to observe
rather than participate, as my physical and psychological
energies slowly dwindled.

During the early 1980s, a good part of my emotional
existence was still tied up with Aminu. While he was alive
he was living out my fantasies, as though he were my personal representative on the power front. He was acting as I
hoped I would, had I been in his shoes.

I think Aminu had sensed some of this and we had felt that

much closer as a result. Our discussions were a give and take, with our ideas coinciding more often than otherwise. My ability to synthesize from his experiences could give him some ammunition he could use when he returned to the political wars, and these intimate but interrupted contacts enabled me to better perceive the conditions under which he worked and to apply them to my own life.

Yet during those last months, he seemed to become more and more removed, with events and his responses to them slipping out of control. At the time he took his last trip to New York City, less than six months before he died, he was being set upon by ill-health as well as by those around him – and he seemed to realize this without admitting it to anyone, even himself.

❧

Having reached another crossroads, I had to find some way to reinforce my lifelong drive toward activism and its inherent optimism. I had always thought one's efforts to help improve the lot of people would provide the bridge between a man and his family and friends to the outer circle – all those others out there. Hanging on to this, but now shorn of my belief in Aminu-ism, I struggled.

Thus began a personal inventory of, first, the philosophical underpinnings of my life to this time, and then a review of the path over which my convictions through the years had taken me.

I had come to believe that no one could participate in the on-going struggle for the human soul and mind without first solving the conflicts within oneself. How could a writer, politician, philosopher or sociologist presume to suggest a guide book for society to follow, when he or she is still attempting to find the solutions? Yet society moves on, with one set of ruling principles or another. Where do these rules come from?

There are those – Marxists, clerics, for example – who presumably have answered the basic problems within themselves and who have subsequently set forth to guide others. They have discovered what is real to them, and all that remains is to apply this knowledge to each aspect of life, minute or grand, and then to lead others to the reality they have discovered. In my youth, I was one of those. With my Little Red Book in hand I bravely set out to face the world, protected from all evil. The goodness in my heart would ultimately be matched by the goodness of others. If a match was not found, well just explain, teach, help, until the true light would pierce the darkness. We boycotted the high school lunchroom because the principal was siphoning off funds, and we met in dark cellars on hard benches. If we were to win others over, we, the disciples, had to be the smartest, most honest and most able.

It seems peculiar to remember one's teens in ideological terms, but the psychological and emotional tensions inherent in that developmental stage were never insurmountable barriers for me. I guess the stresses were there all right, but once I had seen the light and found the all-encompassing system, everything had its solution. Time, knowledge, experience, understanding were all on my side. The logic of it was overpowering, even before I knew the meaning of the word "philosophy."

There is yet another group that renounces all attempts to find order in our society, other than the order of the jungle. The thinking goes, "What pleases me is correct and therefore it is the same for others." This group believes the rules of society should be limited to arbitrating the conflicts which might and do arise.

And then there are the pragmatists, who make up the rules as they go along, guided only by a broad sense of what

With Mary at 65th birthday, 1983

Mary, Nancy and Fred at 50th wedding anniversary, 1994

is right and what is wrong. It is from all these groups that the organizers of society arise, for those who somehow never find the answers within themselves will never be able to lead society.

On the face of it, the answer to this ethical dilemma seems fairly simple if we consider that morality is a concept we have fashioned ourselves; that we live for ourselves and are not the pawns of some ideal force that requires us to live for some greater purpose. What will benefit humanity and make happiness for ourselves and others, is good. The complications arise when the social good is perceived to be in conflict with the individual good, or if "What makes me happy does not make you happy."

⚜

When I look back, I think of the mid 1950s as a turning point. Half my life was over and I was as engaged in our society, as up to my neck in living my life as anyone could possibly be. Before then it had been clear who were the good guys and who the bad. I was helping to change the world, wrestling the power from the exploiters and putting it in the hands of the exploited. I was comfortable in knowing all the basic answers and firmly aligned with the forces of good.

I had minor successes, as well as setbacks. No matter that we progressive were at the periphery of society trying to batter down its gates, far from the principal plazas, the gathering places of the mainstream. We had an established direction and, most important, we were moving forward hand in hand. We had grown up during the Great Depression, accompanied by the revelation and promise of a new society. Fascism, the scourge of our century, had emerged as a counter-force to this brave new world of the future. Our choice to become active partisans of anti-fascism dominated our hearts and minds. We were having an effect, we were masters of our fate.

Then, in 1953, the world according Karl Marx – and Alan Feinstein – fell apart. Thereafter, I searched more than ten years for a substitute for the moral certitude I had lived with, continuing on the face of things to function much the same as I had been, but reduced to isolated, separate, tactical responses to the more glaring of our social failings, no longer geared toward the cohesive force that had unified my efforts.

I had to find a new world viewpoint to conform to my old value system, one that would leave me with some justification for past activities, which I knew deep down to be moral, meaningful, and well-intentioned.

Rationally, I had to learn to fit my activities into a pragmatic world, dropping my dependence on an ideological framework, and applying my broad concept of right and wrong as best I could. But the emotional void remained. My core of satisfaction had to be found only within my conscience and judgment, bereft of a central overall plan. That had to do.

These progressive with their middle-class fat and radicalism stuck with the plan – through all the harsh McCarthy years, the prosecutions, trials and ostracism – and fell away in large part only after the revelations of the Twentieth Congress of the USSR, when the moral basis of their attachment to a cause was destroyed.

That was when the shining beacon of the future had begun to tarnish for me. I saw a pattern of life emerging, wonderful though it might be personally, with great children growing rapidly, loving wife pointing the way for a sensual, vital love of life as it is, not as it might someday be; yet I could only continue in my rut.

It was a huge leap from that unsatisfactory and unsettled

state of affairs to my Africa phase. But when it did come about, the gnawing at the pit of my stomach lessened. I had found a focus – political, exciting, adventuresome and all-consuming. In Aminu Kano and what he represented, there was renewal. He was everything I could fantasize for myself: his ideas, actions, dedication were mine.

Writing his biography tied our bond closer and closer. The long hours of interviewing gave me deeper insights into his thinking, and I even felt that my own analyses and perceptions were being recognized. I was once again making a dent. This Africa connection kept me going thereafter, for two decades, with new challenges and new directions. Yet through it all, the gnawing would return.

Aminu's death was more crucial to my thinking than I had realized. Aside from the obviously horrendous loss of my standard bearer, it came at a shattering time. His party had been torn into shreds with only Aminu's towering figure remaining. And then he was gone. Within eight months the whole shaky government apparatus with which he had been trying so hard to work had collapsed.

Collapsing with it was my sense of history, of progress, of believing that individuals could make a difference and still remain in control of their destiny. I was set adrift. History could no longer represent for me the slow, unceasing movement in the right direction, no matter how imperceptible.

The most difficult reconciliation of all is the ultimate recognition that humanists have never run society for any length of time. The not-so-silent majority has its day every day. It takes great inner strength, disengagement, a low-consciousness level, farsightedness, or some combination of all, for the principled to continue to retain their faith in the ultimate victory of good.

⚜

That realization has not been easy to live with, but my assessment of my own role in life clearly is not a new one. Notes I made to myself back in 1964 sounds much like the ones I wrote in the late 1980s and early 1990s.

Without repeating my concerns, I can say that this nebulous tie to society and need to find social meaning in my life still dominates my mind. Most people find their social ties through their work, without consciously caring to analyze what the struggle is about. It is why men and women fear retirement or loss of job, why women in mid-life cast about for new roles when their children fly the coop.

My lifelong bent toward activism, however, seems to be pretty much spent at this stage. My abiding interest in writing has served as a vehicle through which I find social connection. Nevertheless, I find it very difficult to initiate another project that can keep me off the unending merry-go-round of shows and social visits – all of which can have their place if a central focus for personal expression is maintained.

There is a certain desperation that accompanies the realization that the future is upon me, and that instead of dwelling on these cosmic thoughts I should be searching through my past to look for some significance that could be passed on to others.

Perhaps my concentration should be more on the present with its immediate satisfactions, as is the case with most of my contemporaries. But the enigma remains for one whose present has always consisted of pecking away at future goals and whose illusions have continued to tantalize him, always with the hope that his efforts will have an effect, no matter how slight.

༺❀༻

Alan, with Mary
and Nancy when
Nancy received
her PhD, 1982

With Karen and Nancy,
West Virginia, 1983

With Fred at Fred's swearing-in
ceremony as General Counsel of
National Labor Relations Board, 1993

As my golden years approached, the more involved I become with examining my inner worth, and the less taken was I with the outer world. But I continued to think about my continuing obsession with the never-never world and its inability to organize itself sensibly.

Such pessimistic philosophical search for meaning undoubtedly contributed to my dispiritedness following the dismal results of our own 1988 elections in the USA, but I realized my response was part of a continuum. If anything, over the years the extent of my discontent seems to grow.

My occasional bouts of despondency actually represent a deep seated contradiction in the face of my generally trouble-free life. Neither my psyche nor my soma have ever been seriously challenged. Yet uneasiness has gnawed at me for as long as I can remember.

From time to time an ennui returns, sometimes strong, sometimes just subliminally in the background, ready to emerge upon the slightest change in direction of the political winds. There are few causes that could bring me back into action, that might help revive my deep liking for and faith in people.

Meanwhile I slog along, each day taking a wee bit more out of me than the last. I complain that I don't have enough time to relax, only to find that when I manage to squeeze out a few moments I waste them just as likely as not, or find time to scribble notes of self-complaint about the hole in my life that remains unfilled. The distress I feel for human kind is shoveled into that hole, disappears from view until it appears once again in another shape.

Now consolation comes with the realization that civilization, such as it is, will go on even though I won't. With the end of the cold war, nuclear holocaust becomes far less likely. My lifelong concerns will have to be faced by our children, and they won't have any more answers than I have.

It is satisfying to see both our children carrying on with their parents' social concerns, without being burdened by our political baggage. I find lately that my fully independent existence is turning more toward living a goodly part of it through my son and daughter.

I am justly proud of both of them, their spouses and children, and almost feel as though I'm acting on the world through all of them. Though a quiet contemplative father, and a good listener, at this stage in my life, I seem, however, to want perhaps to share more of their lives than I get. Or at least to have my listening yield more detail.

I also sense some deference on their part to my role in shaping their lives, which in turn gives me much pleasure. I've been learning (I hope) not to be too disappointed when our contacts are not more revealing, knowing that the deepest truths, if spoken at all, come softly murmured – or through shared silence. I still find it difficult though, to realize that most of the warmth we share is that of memories, not ongoing experience.

CHAPTER NINETEEN

REFLECTING

---

*"This act of recording bestows me with a feeling of
an enduring connection with the world."*

Most of us who reach our seventies in reasonably good shape
are concerned that the future has come and gone, that our
lives are pretty much over, with the remaining years a kind of
bonus that we somehow don't quite know how to deal with.
While we are trying to figure this out, the days and years slip
by. Today we're seventy, tomorrow we're seventy-one, and
another year has gone.

In the absence of a time clock to punch or deep involvement with a work schedule on a regular basis, the days are
consumed with small chores. It's a lucky day now when I can
say that my senses were stimulated enough to mark that
particular day as memorable. This is a far cry from the act of

cutting into a long range plan, with something concrete and measurable having been chipped away that very day.

When there are no week-ends to mark one's weekly progress; when one's thoughts get swallowed up in the time-less progression of day following night; when one has a past to look back on, and a present to relax in, the future all but disappears – and we stop buying green bananas.

In the face of all this free and unscheduled time, it is a strong mind that can keep the valves open indefinitely until they are shut off for good, and yet, until that moment, never indulge the thought that one's time doesn't go on forever. Who knows at what age the future begins to disappear, or when the juices dry up and one becomes mostly reactive rather than an initiator or creator.

⚜

These days about the most relaxing and reassuring spot in the world is right on our back lawn in Mohegan. Hasn't changed much. At any rate, it's always comfortable to sit there and stare into space, to read, write, solve a crossword puzzle, or just do anything that comes to mind. No chores, no daily *New York Times* or Africana material.

Nevertheless there is something to say for returning to a spot of beauty year after year and comfortably slipping into the familiar chaise-longue, tasting the unimpeded mix of sight, sound and smell, away from the usual work-a-day sen-sate world. The ability to observe nature all around us is ever present.

I sit here often, writing notes, quietly listening to the gentle mix of natural and human sounds: the crickets, or cicadas, the bird calls, a distant car speeding by, coupled with the most pleasant of man-made sounds, classical music. And though I can go out anytime, chat and enjoy the interface with assorted friends and relatives, I am always eager for a return to myself.

While sitting at my desk, the small and large batches of time usually slip away hardly noticed. Yes things get done, bills get paid, notes and letters written; I make diary entries, work at the word processor. But when all is said and done, and the day, the hours, have disappeared, there is disappointment at how little I have to show for it.

When taking to writing, one steps back to observe and pretty much remove oneself from participation. Is that a form of separation? Perhaps that is why I am drawn to the pen. Even when on rare occasions I wander timelessly and agelessly through crowded and busy streets, getting a sense of all the other worlds passing me by without my knowledge or consent, as though I no longer exist, I end up with that same feeling that even these observations must be recorded someplace, somehow.

Is it a form of escape into luxuriant solitude that gives me solace in my latter-day choice of writing as a primary connection to the world? After enough passive passage of time, of the imbibing of knowledge via the written word, I still find myself incomplete.

The knowledge that I acquire, such as it is, dies with me if not imparted to others, and that realization leaves a deep internal void. Is it just the desperate need to create, to convey something to others, coupled with the presumption that I have something worthwhile to record?

It is something of a thrill to have someone read and react to my jottings, but there is also fulfillment on a lesser scale, but fulfillment nevertheless, in the simple act of recording and ultimately rereading at some future date.

I suppose, if analyzed, this act of recording bestows me with a feeling of an enduring connection with the world. I have never enjoyed the thought that I am just passing through, like everyone else. Those once around me who have already gone through this final rite of passage are remembered by the remaining few who were in immediate day-to-day contact with them. But here it is their presence that is missed, not so much their active contributions.

⁓

As the days and months roll by, I find myself thinking more and more about the passage of time, the aging process, and my own reaction to both. In the midst of all this, death hovers over my consciousness like a cloud. Not threatening, not feared, but ever present. It is just time closing in on me, gradually, almost imperceptibly. It is a sense of the finiteness of life, its impending conclusion – -and irreversibility.

I see my own experience as that of a frustrated intellectual who somehow had high, and perhaps unrealistic, aspirations, and seemed therefore unable to realize them. This gap between aspiration and achievement leaves me disappointed, though I never cast anyone around me as being responsible for my own inadequacies. They are all internal.

I find it impossible to modify these aspirations, but realize at this time that the autumn and winter of my life aren't likely to yield any more than did the spring and summer. If I want to relax and enjoy my good fortune, I had better learn to live with the chasm.

I seem to approach that goal successfully for limited periods of time, but then those unfulfilled aims begin to intrude themselves, leaving me fidgety and never fully comfortable with the good life. The end will come when it does and the thought of it doesn't frighten me, but then how about all those unrealized dreams?

⁓

It is amazing how guilt feelings permeate these cosmic thoughts. Why, when we look around at all the tragedy and near tragedy befalling those who surround us, have we escaped unscathed? How many funeral elegies must we deliver or listen to before we are no longer the subject, but become the object?

Yet through all the guilt brought on by survival comes a warm glow of reminiscence of a life well spent. I can surely depart anytime along the line, without fear or regret – and I hope that until then I can empathize and try to share some of our good fortune with those around us who can use it.

I reassure myself that it's not the result of one's efforts, but the process and motivation that counts. The awareness of some seventy-plus years of a healthy, eventful, productive and love-filled life leaves me reasonably content and ready for its inevitable conclusion.

⚜

And then we come upon a beautiful caressing spring sunshine that just cries our for contact with nature's annual festival of rebirth and growth, but is now attainable only in brief spurts, always limited and continually interrupted by bouts of fatigue or an aching back, relieved only in seated repose.

During these moments of repose, thoughts of my social role become less important. Whether dawdling or just staring into space, whether I'm connected or not, matters little at such times. My connection to the world just seems to rest on my very being. I'm part of this magnificent whole and acutely conscious of it.

My age doesn't seem to matter then either. Only an observable slowing of the pace. The moments of tranquillity and peace are not that frequent, but they sure are relished more. And they seem to provide a logical continuity to the themes and values of my life while coincidentally giving me some sense of the ageless self.

⁂

Where I am today is compounded of past personal decisions and present attitudes within the parameters of the value system that evolved over the years, influenced by family, peers, work and extracurricular experiences, and of course the effect of chance.

Youth with its activism and sense of time infinite ultimately yields to an awareness of the winding down and closing in of the future. With my inability to hate comes a lessening of the more positive emotions such as joy, enthusiasm and passion. Present instead is more of a tendency toward repose, accompanied by a seeming powerlessness and inability to influence events.

It is odd that the sense of stability and lack of sharp emotional peaks and valleys over my lifetime somehow left me wanting. It certainly wasn't for lack of involvement or concern. I was always groping and reaching for unfathomed heights, but my search was cast in social terms.

Through my responses to events or just plain luck, my life was devoid of any personal struggle. Blessed with healthy, capable wife and children; secure in the knowledge that my relationship with family and friends has always been quite good; that I could always earn a living as a successful professional, I had to look elsewhere for struggle and found it in the eternal war against the abuses of the wielders of power.

Even at this stage in my life, some passion is needed just to push back the fall of the curtain. The confidence that the world can be changed if only I put forth that additional ounce of effort is dwindling with the passing of the years, but my need to remain a socially involved participant is not.

Then have I finally learned to accept the obvious? To take my own personal good fortune and run with it, not letting the state of society distress me so? To join as best I can with the good people around me, minority or majority, to move forward on one level or another as the times dictate?

Will I be able to put my brief remaining years to good advantage, knowing that whatever struggles and movements I have participated in over my lifetime will continue ad eternum? I can hope when my children, and then again their children face these same problems, they face them squarely and find themselves aligned with the Aminu's of the world, and yes, the Alan's too.

And when I finally appear before those pearly gates, will I be able to answer honestly the ultimate question that St. Peter, the heavenly concierge, asks all potential residents, *"Which side were you on?"* with *"The right side."*

If I can so answer, will that also serve as my path to that elusive goal, the immortality we all seek?

With Mary, 1995

Feinstein clan, 1994

EPILOGUE

My love died on December 29, 1995 after a four-month illness. My wonderful life died with him.

We had a very special memorial for him on Martin Luther
King Day at the United Nations Chapel in New York, with his
friends and family there to say good-bye to him.

The many people who were there and who stood up to
honor his life and his memory, reflected the broad and beautiful spectrum of Alan's life and interests. Among them were
former New York Mayor David Dinkins, Nigerian Ambassador
to the United Nations Nations Ibrahim Gambari, former U.S.
Ambassador to Nigeria Donald Easum, friends Milton Jaffe
and Elizabeth McLaurin, son Fred and daughter Nancy and
grandniece Heidi Adelman. Son-in-law Glenn Shor led the
Kaddish, while daughter-in-law Karen Collins sang an old

union song that seemed to speak directly to Alan's life. Our family friend, Travis Gering, played the flute.

The noted Nigerian novelist and poet Chinua Achebe ended the memorial with a quote from another noted poet, William Shakespeare:

"His life was gentle and the elements so mixed in him. That nature might stand up and say to all the world, `This was a man`."

In Alan's memory we've established a foundation to create the Aminu Kano Study Center in Kano, Nigeria. Contributions may be sent to Aminu Kano Study Center, c/o Donald Easum, 801 West End Avenue, Apt 33A, New York, NY 10025

–Mary Kotick Feinstein

AFTERWORD

I met Alan and Mary Feinstein some thirty years ago. During these years, I made it a point, whenever I was in New York, to visit these good friends.

Alan and I shared the same passion for Africa. This passion was translated in long discussions on the problems of this continent that suffered so much, from slavery, to colonial domination. Today Africa is in danger of being marginalized by "afropessimism" and the globalization of the economy.

It is through men such as Alan Feinstein that the world learned to know Africa, its leaders, its aspirations and its disappointment. For, if the future of Africa depends, first and foremost, on the Africans themselves, it also depends on men and women of good will who, through their interest in our continent, have learned to love it, and have thus helped make it known to the public at large.

I am pleased to pay tribute to Alan Feinstein for his love of Africa in general, and Nigeria in particular, as well as for his extensive, profound dialogue with the great African leader Aminu Kano.

BOUTROS BOUTROS-GHALI
Former Deputy Prime Minister for Foreign Affairs of Egypt
Former Secretary-General of the United Nations Organization